MW01035890

Disciple

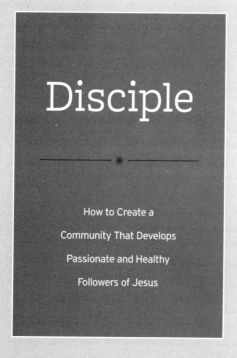

Disciple

How to Create a

Community That Develops

Passionate and Healthy

Followers of Jesus

Chuck Lawless

Thom S. Rainer, Series Editor

TYNDALE
MOMENTUM®

A Tyndale nonfiction imprint

Library of Congress Cataloging-in-Publication Data

A catalog record for this book is available from the Library of Congress.

ISBN 978-1-4964-6464-4

Printed in the United States of America

28	27	26	25	24	23	22
7	6	5	4	3	2	1

To Pam,

my partner in all I do

and

to all the men

who have invested in me

over the years

Contents

Introduction   1

CHAPTER 1:   The Problem   9

CHAPTER 2:   What Exactly Is a Disciple?   29

CHAPTER 3:   Getting Started as a Disciplemaking Church   49

CHAPTER 4:   Next Steps   67

Conclusion   89

Notes   93

About the Author   99

Introduction

I WANT TO start by asking you three questions.

First, how would you rate your church in the areas of worship, evangelism, fellowship, discipleship, prayer, and ministry? Which area would you rate the highest? The lowest?

Next, which of these areas in your church (if any) would you consider healthy? Unhealthy?

Finally, which area do you think most churches have consistently ranked the lowest for the twenty-plus years I've been doing this type of survey?

I have consulted with churches for almost three decades. For most of that time, I've used a 160-question Church Health Survey (now the Know Your Church Report) to learn a church's perception of its own health in the same six areas mentioned above.[1] We have used the survey with churches of all sizes, in several denominations, all around the country. Almost without exception, churches have reported that they are weakest in the areas of evangelism and discipleship. I cannot remember the last church I surveyed where that was not the case.

Those findings probably shouldn't be surprising. Depending on the study, anywhere from 65 percent to 85 percent of Protestant churches in the United States have plateaued or are declining.[2]

They are not reaching nonbelievers, nor are they discipling believers. A joint 2015 discipleship study by the Barna Group and The Navigators confirmed these concerns.[3] And I suspect these issues have not improved much since that study:

- Church leaders admit that churches are not discipling new and young leaders very well.
- Participation in discipleship activities such as Sunday school, spiritual mentoring, or group Bible studies tends to be weak.
- Church leaders say that busyness and a lack of commitment to discipleship are the two biggest barriers to developing strong discipleship strategies.
- Programmatic approaches to discipleship have not been effective.
- A lack of equipped leaders willing to disciple others is a significant issue.
- Overall, a lack of priority for discipleship at the individual and corporate levels has led to general apathy about spiritual growth.
- Most churches have no means to evaluate whether their members are growing spiritually.

Clearly, we have not produced communities of passionate followers of Jesus. And we have a long way to go if we want to grow disciplemaking churches. At best, our discipleship efforts have been superficial.[4] As I've surveyed churches, I've discovered at least six reasons that churches don't disciple well. Do any of them describe your church?

1. **Many church leaders—pastors included—have never been discipled.** That was true of me when I started pastoring more than forty years ago. You're not alone if that's your story too. If we knew the truth, I suspect the number of pastors who have not been intentionally discipled would be surprisingly high.

2. **In many cases, church leaders find more reward in reporting new believers.** Some denominations, for example, ask for reports about new converts. Some give recognition to congregations that apparently evangelize well. Sometimes we pastors like to talk about our church's good evangelistic numbers. What we seldom report, though, is the number of believers intentionally being discipled in our congregations. The number is often low, and the incentive for strategically reviewing this number is equally low.

3. **Discipleship is tough, tiring, messy work.** To disciple well means you have to walk with people in their everyday faith. You must be willing to encourage and lead through defeats and victories. You must be patient but persistent. Sometimes it's just easier not to do it.

4. **We've reduced discipleship to a series of courses.** Discipleship is life-on-life guidance; it's not simply completing a number of courses (and sometimes earning some kind of certificate). As an educator, I'm not opposed to curriculum as part of discipleship. But courses alone are not enough to produce devoted disciples of Jesus.

5. **We leave little room for struggle and growth in new believers.** Instead, we expect them to just "get it" and grow in Christlikeness almost immediately. When they

don't grow quickly enough, too often we judge them before we help them. We might grant grace to new believers on the mission field who struggle with leaving behind their non-Christian worldview and habits, but we offer little grace to our new-believer neighbors who face the same struggles.

6. **We don't always teach the high demands of the gospel.** When we fail to talk about things like Jesus' requirement that we deny ourselves and take up our cross (Luke 9:23), we teach a watered-down gospel. Consequently, people don't see the need for someone to walk with them in true discipleship.[5]

What I didn't include in this list is the problem underlying most of these issues: Many churches simply haven't given much intentional thought to disciplemaking. They may have tried some programs, but any success was short-lived. Church leaders may have read books on the topic, but reading a book is quite different from implementing a strategy. They may have had conversations with other leaders about becoming a disciplemaking church, but the initiative ended with the conversations.

On the other hand, leaders of strong discipleship ministries (called *discipleship exemplars* in the Barna/Navigator study) said two factors contribute the most to strong discipleship ministries: (1) support from senior leadership, and (2) a clear plan for developing disciples. My own research has shown that when leaders do not publicly prioritize discipleship, their churches won't either. They may talk the talk, but anything less than obvious support from leadership will hinder a church's discipleship strategy.

Discipleship exemplars in the Barna/Navigators study also

pointed to the significance of a clearly articulated strategy, though church leaders still recognized a need for much improvement in this area. Strong discipleship ministries know what their purpose is, understand where they want the ministry to go, and have a clear plan to get there. But it's not easy to find a church that has developed and implemented a clear pathway for believers to grow to be more and more like Christ. Few churches have mapped out an intentional path to maturity.

It's not that churches do *nothing*. They plan, but they don't always strategize.

Christian growth is often equated with "church activity," and there's usually a lot of activity going on. The problem is that busy church members remain undiscipled members because the church has no cohesive plan of spiritual formation. They are "doing stuff," but without the intentionality necessary for discipleship.

I liken the situation to puzzle pieces lying on the floor when no one knows what the puzzle is supposed to look like.[6] All the pieces may be there, but they won't be properly connected until someone can provide a picture of the completed puzzle. Sometimes a few of the pieces are missing, in which case the puzzle will be incomplete until those final pieces are found and put in place. A lack of clear goals in making disciples leads only to frustrating, ineffective, and inefficient efforts to put the puzzle together.

Nevertheless, more and more churches are at least raising questions about how they might disciple better. Particularly among younger churches, there's a desire to correct this problem—and that's the focus of this book. I want to help church leaders at least begin to think about the completed picture of the puzzle. If your church needs to tackle that issue, I pray this book will help and encourage you.

Our Road Map

I don't know what leadership position you hold in your church, but I hope you've picked up this book because you recognize the need to make disciples. I believe this topic matters, and I look forward to walking with you through the next steps. Here's a brief overview of where we're going.

Chapter 1 will help you further understand the discipleship problem and begin to evaluate your own life and church. I will challenge you to consider what a disciple should look like in your church.

Chapter 2 tackles the most basic question we must answer if we want to make disciples: *What exactly is a disciple of Jesus?* Others much wiser than I have answered this question, and we will use their insights to inform our perspective. Thom Rainer and Ed Stetzer, for example, define disciples as "those who trust Christ alone for salvation and follow God in a maturing process of faith and life."[7] Pastor J. T. English views a disciple as "someone who has received the identity of the Triune God through baptism and who follows the teaching of Christ through obedience."[8] For me, a disciple is simply a follower of Christ in the process of being conformed to his image. Discipleship thus moves us in the direction of being more Christlike.

Chapter 3 focuses on first steps toward leading and growing a disciplemaking church. My goal in this chapter is for you to *start somewhere* and *do something* in this process.

Chapter 4 will guide you through additional steps to create disciples, beginning with identifying who a "disciple" is for your church.

The conclusion will leave you with a final challenge as you tackle the task of discipleship.

Along the way, I will ask you to evaluate your church's discipleship efforts and reflect on the ways in which you yourself have been discipled. I encourage you not to skip over these questions, but to prayerfully look at your life and your church. Honest assessment is an important first step toward improvement.

I want to help you become a disciple and make other disciples. I'm honored you're joining me!

CHAPTER 1

The Problem

Janie is a member of First Church. She became a Christ-follower at age fifteen when a neighbor talked to her about salvation. The whole story was new to her. Her parents were not believers. She had never read the Bible. No one had talked to her about Jesus before her neighbor did—but it all made sense when Janie heard it.

She attended her neighbor's church, where she was baptized soon after her conversion. It was a significant day in her life when family and friends witnessed her taking this big step. Her church family rejoiced with her. Everything changed when Janie met Jesus—even for a fifteen-year-old. At least for a while.

Within months, Janie had dropped out of church. Church members wondered what had happened to her, but nobody followed up with her. After all, it was not uncommon for excited new church members to lose their passion over time. The congregation had seen it happen before. And they would see it happen again. Their church had no strategy in place to guide new believers to become devoted disciples of Jesus, and Janie was just the latest casualty from that failure.

Down the street at Second Church is Patrick, who has been a part of the church since before he was born. His grandparents were charter members, and his parents were stalwarts in the congregation. They taught Patrick and his siblings about Jesus almost every day. As an eight-year-old, when Patrick began to understand his own sinfulness, he chose to follow Jesus on his own.

That was many years ago. Today, Patrick is a leader in the church. He facilitates a small group, helps count the offering, and serves as an usher. Most church members recognize him as a man of God—an example for others in the congregation and the community.

What they don't know is that Patrick really struggles in his faith walk. His Bible reading is sporadic, at best. Prayer happens only when he faces something he can't handle on his own. Fasting is nonexistent. If you asked Patrick to explain basic biblical doctrine, he couldn't go far in that direction. He has not shared the gospel with anyone in years. Actually, he never has.

Only he knows the ongoing battles he has with particular sins in his life. No matter how hard he tries to overcome them, he experiences defeat almost daily. He surely can't tell anyone, though, because the church family sees him as a godly leader. It's easier to hide his sin than risk his reputation. Though Patrick is a leader in his church, he's actually still an immature believer.

How did this situation happen? Second Church has had no plan in place to disciple new believers, raise up leaders, and equip them for the work of ministry (Ephesians 4:11-12). Instead, they assume that every church member who attends a small group and the worship service will connect all the dots on their own and grow as a believer. That seldom happens, however, and Patrick is only one of several underdeveloped leaders in their church.

Across town is Third Church, where Jay and Beth serve faithfully together. They met in another church, where they also were married, but they've been attending Third for almost ten years. They joined the church when Jay's job brought them to the area. In fact, they searched for a church home even while they looked for a new residence. In no way did they want to lose the focus of their Christian commitment in a time of transition.

They quickly knew that Third Church was the place for them—but even they were surprised by what they found there. Though they had attended several churches over the years of their marriage, they had never seen a church with a deliberate disciplemaking strategy as developed as Third's was. It didn't take long for them to realize that, although their previous churches had been comfortable fits for them, they had not really helped them grow with intentionality. They were good churches, but not strong disciplemaking churches.

Third Church was different. Different from most other churches, in fact. Third Church had a plan to move *non*believers to *new* believers to *growing* believers to *reproducing* believers.[1] They had a plan to make disciples.

Third Church is a community of passionate, healthy, and growing followers of Christ—the kind of church that is the goal of this book. But because so many churches aren't like Third Church, let's first think about problems that develop when a church has a weak or nonexistent plan for making disciples:

1. **Biblical illiteracy.** Listening to sermons and attending small groups are great for learning the Word of God, yet

many believers who do both still know very little of the Word. Strong discipleship *deepens* our knowledge and helps us *apply* biblical truths.

2. **Faith struggles.** This is what happens when we don't really know the Word of God. That lack of knowledge makes it difficult to trust God when we face our own obstacles and impossibilities.

3. **Inward focus.** Churches that don't do a good job of discipleship typically default to an inward focus; that is, their attention is more on themselves than on others. Only an intentional strategy to direct believers to the living Word—that is, to Jesus—and the Great Commission in the written word (Matthew 28:18-20) can change that focus. That's what discipleship does.

4. **Unsaved church members.** Some church members who've never truly repented and followed Jesus are convinced they're saved. They don't really know the gospel, nor do they know what the gospel demands. A lack of discipleship doesn't help here.

5. **Unqualified leaders.** Churches often select ministry leaders based on their faithfulness and willingness. Both characteristics matter, but poor discipleship sometimes leads to faithful, willing, yet unqualified people in leadership positions.

6. **Continual whiners.** Complaining is almost inevitable when discipleship is lacking. Baby believers remain babies unless someone teaches them to feed themselves. Babies who never grow up, but who nevertheless are put in positions of leadership, often become whiners.

7. **Sin struggles.** One reason believers wrestle continually with sin is that they have never been taught how to deal with temptation. It's tough to win a battle when you don't understand the battle you face or the armor you should be wearing (Ephesians 6:10-17).

8. **Weak families.** When we assume that couples and parents will simply "get it right" apart from the church's teaching, we're often proven wrong. Healthy Christian marriages and strong, God-centered parenting are the results of good discipleship.

9. **Powerless churches.** God's blessing falls on churches that walk with him in obedience and pray to him in dependence. Undiscipled people, however, seldom do either one—and the church goes through the motions without the power of God.

10. **Generational problems.** When one generation is not discipled, the next generation also pays a price. The unhealthy, unbiblical cycle continues, and the church may suffer for decades.[2]

Frankly, at this point in the book, you might be feeling discouraged. I hope that's not the case. It's certainly not my goal. I believe in the local church, and I've seen congregations begin to address these issues in healthy, productive ways. I want your church to be one of those churches. For now, though, take a minute to evaluate your church. Then continue with me as I tell you why this topic matters so much to me.

If I Could Do It All Again

I was a member of only one church before I started pastoring at age twenty. I became a Christ-follower in seventh grade, after a classmate told me about Jesus. I am forever grateful to that church in southwestern Ohio for giving me an unwavering belief and trust in the Word of God. They grounded me in the authority of the Word, and that commitment has influenced my life ever since. I would not be where I am today were it not for that congregation helping me get started in my Christian walk.

At the same time, the church didn't have an intentional disciple-making strategy. They had worship services, Sunday school, small group training—all significant components of a church that wants to make disciples—but they didn't strategically tie the programs together into a cohesive discipleship plan. They had the important puzzle pieces, but those pieces were scattered about. Nobody had put them together in such a way that we could *see* the goal.

Instead, this church was like Second Church in the opening section of this chapter. They assumed that attendance and participation in all the church's programs and activities would naturally result in faithful, growing disciples of Christ. That *did* happen at times, but it was coincidental rather than intentional. In my case, it only happened so far—and not far enough.

I was a teenage guy trying to live a Christian life in a non-Christian home with few Christian role models. I did my best in Bible reading and prayer. I evangelized a lot, but not always well. Sin struggles—and defeats—were all too common. My relationship with my parents wasn't great, and I didn't know how to change that. I was an infant believer trying to feed myself and teach myself to walk—and that doesn't work very well. When I later started teaching Sunday school, I was more excited about the task than I was prepared or qualified for it. I desperately needed someone to disciple me directly.

Moreover, I was not as ready as I needed to be when I started pastoring at age twenty. Still, a small congregation in Ohio, who knew me through a previous pastor, called me to lead them. They graciously loved me enough to let me grow through my mistakes. And I made mistakes. A lot of them, actually. I made so many mistakes that I can only thank the Lord the congregation did not give up on me.

Looking back, I greatly regret that I didn't know how to disciple the new believers the Lord gave us. Evangelistic zeal marked our congregation, and we regularly rejoiced as God saved people we loved. Over two years, we saw more than one hundred nonbelievers choose to follow Christ. Almost every Sunday, we reported on a new brother or sister in Christ. To say that excitement reigned when we gathered for worship would be an understatement—but we had no plan to help these new believers grow.

Here's what that meant: We had a lot of baby believers in our congregation who were excited about Jesus. They wanted to know more, especially after they learned something new from the Scriptures. They were hungry for more teaching, more training, more challenge. I just didn't know how to lead in that direction.

Instead, I focused on reaching more people without developing the ones we had already reached.

You can probably figure out what happened. We still needed leaders in the church, so we sometimes appointed believers who weren't ready for their assignment. They loved the Lord and the church, but they weren't always spiritually equipped for the work. They honestly thought they were, though, because our congregation had set them apart to lead. They were, in many ways, baby believers leading other baby believers. As I reflect, our criteria for selecting leaders—they only had to be faithful to the church and be willing to serve—should have been just starting points for selection rather than the ending point.

To my regret, several of those young believers did not remain faithful for long. Some disappeared so soon after their baptism that we wondered whether they had ever been believers in the first place. Others remained faithful until they faced a life crisis with insufficient faith to handle it. Some battled temptation so unsuccessfully that they always lived in defeat. Still others stayed as long as I was the pastor, but the transition period between pastors gave them a convenient opportunity to walk away. That's what happens to baby believers given little guidance and support: They wander.

To this day, I grieve that leadership failure on my part. We had passionate followers of Christ in that church, but they weren't always healthy; in fact, their passion often waned when life got hard. They didn't know how to remain faithful and joyous, because I had not discipled them well. I'm writing this book to help others avoid that same mistake.

I'm glad to say that my commitment to discipleship improved in the second church I pastored, though I still had much room to grow. We had some intentional structure to our small groups, and our chosen curriculum led to specific discipling goals we had set.

Our deacons helped establish a new member's class designed to start a believer in the right direction toward growth. We worked hard to understand and live by biblical standards in selecting leaders. We didn't answer all the questions well, and we sometimes talked about discipleship more than we did it—but at least we began to ask together, "What does it take to be a disciple of Jesus?"

It wasn't until I was a young seminary professor that I more directly tackled that significant question. My journey took a focused turn when I had the privilege of having dinner with Dr. Robert Coleman, author of the bestselling book *The Master Plan of Evangelism.*[3] As I write these words, Dr. Coleman has been investing in young believers for more than sixty years. He had a mentee with him when I first met him, and I recently heard him speak of a group of men he still meets with every Saturday—and he's now in his nineties! He continues to live like Jesus.

That night at dinner twenty-five years ago, Dr. Coleman challenged me: "Chuck, if you want your ministry to last beyond *you*, you need to start investing in young men now so they'll be disciples of Christ." He spoke with such passion, experience, and wisdom that I knew I must pay attention to his challenge. I needed to become a disciplemaker—which meant I would have to define the term *disciple* and determine what it meant to *be* a disciple and how to *produce* disciples. If I wanted to be a disciplemaker like Jesus, I had to go back to square one.

My goal in this simple book is to help you tackle this task, regardless of your starting point. Whether you are young or old, male or female, lay leader or pastor, you can play a role in helping your church make disciples. If you're just now trying to figure it all out, I pray I can move you in the right direction. If you're a veteran at leading a church that makes disciples, perhaps a nugget or two in this book will help you, as well.

I know I've learned in the process of writing this book. I've been reminded again that, even though I cannot go back and correct my mistakes in ministry, I can keep growing today. Indeed, that's what being a disciple means: growing in our faith, trusting God as he makes us more Christlike.

With Gratitude to a Purpose Driven Study

As a doctoral student in seminary, studying evangelism and church growth, I read Rick Warren's book *The Purpose Driven Church*.[4] Warren, the church planter and pastor of Saddleback Community Church in Orange County, California, tells the story of his church in this popular book. I didn't agree with everything he said, but it played a role in helping me think about making disciples.

To begin, Warren's philosophy of *quantity* and *quality* in the church was quite helpful. It was one of the first books I had read that affirmed numerical growth *and* spiritual growth; in fact, Warren's emphasis on *quality* forced me to remember with some grief my first pastorate, which focused more on *quantity*:

> You do not have to choose between the two. Every church should want both. In fact, an exclusive focus on either quality or quantity will produce an unhealthy church. . . . The fact that many pastors wish to ignore is this: *Quality produces quantity*. A church full of genuinely changed people attracts others. If you study healthy churches you'll discover that when God finds a church that is doing a quality job of winning, nurturing, equipping, and sending out believers, he sends that church plenty of raw material. On the other hand, why would God send a lot of prospects to a church that doesn't know what to do with them?[5]

It's that last question that stopped me in my tracks: Why should God allow us to reach people if we're not prepared to help them grow?

At the same time, Saddleback's "Life Development Process" helped me to see how one church walked believers toward spiritual maturity.[6] The church uses a baseball diamond to diagram their process—moving people from one base to the next—which is built around four specific goals and a series of classes:

- 100 level classes are designed to "lead people to Christ and church membership."
- 200 level classes are intended to "grow people to spiritual maturity."
- 300 level classes "equip people with the skills they need for ministry."
- 400 level classes seek to "enlist people in the worldwide mission of sharing Christ."[7]

It was the intentionality of this process that caught my eye. The church seeks to grow members who complete required trainings, develop strong spiritual habits, exhibit conviction and character, and participate in the mission of God by making other disciples where they live and around the world. Gaining knowledge is only one goal of this process; the larger goal is to lead believers to show their beliefs by their actions. In Rick Warren's words, "Our deeds must be consistent with our creeds."[8]

The process takes time, but the goal is clear: to guide church members to become "Grand Slam Disciples" who complete their training and covenant with the church at each level of training, reaching every base on the diamond in helping the church fulfill the Great Commission.[9] I know churches that speak this same language, but I don't know many who carry out the strategy as well.

Rick Warren also introduced me to "Saddleback Sam," a composite description of the "typical unchurched" person who lived in the church's ministry area, often with his wife, "Saddleback Samantha," and their kids, Steve and Sally.[10] Critics questioned the value of focusing on one type of person in the community, but Warren was simply doing what most good church planters do: researching the people to be reached and summarizing the findings to develop the best means to get the gospel to them. He was seeking to contextualize the church's efforts to reach their community. Other churches have successfully followed this same pattern.

Warren points out that having a composite profile of the community will "make it easier for members of your church to understand who your target is."[11] As I've mentioned before, I'm struck by the fact that we expect missionaries to ask this type of "Who are we trying to reach?" question when they enter a new mission field, but we don't often ask it when the people we're trying to reach live down the block, look like us, and speak our language. Missionaries want to know about cultural mores, religious beliefs, familial relationships, worldview assumptions, power structures, languages spoken, and anything else that might help them reach a people. These are the same kinds of questions *we* need to ask, no matter where we serve.

Knowing who the typical person is in a community should help our churches strategically plan their outreach into those communities. The Great Commission (Matthew 28:18-20) requires that we seek to reach *everyone* around us, and taking the time to identify and understand these people should increase our burden to reach them. Our hearts are more likely to break over lostness when we know the faces and names of those lost people.

EVALUATION FOR YOUR CHURCH
1. Has your church helped you to know who is living in your community—that is, who your Saddleback Sam, Samantha, Steve, and Sally are?
2. In your assessment, how broken is your congregation over the lostness in your community?

The concept of Saddleback Sam, which I found quite helpful when I first read about it, gave rise to another question for me: Once we have identified the people we need to reach, what pathway will we walk with them to help them become devoted disciples of Jesus? We must be able to describe the "disciples" we want to produce through our discipleship process.

Consider this scenario, using the names Dave and Debbie for two nonbelievers who live in your community.[12] They began attending your church at the invitation of one of your church members. It was all new to them, but they kept returning to worship with you. Having heard the gospel, they recently chose to turn to Christ for salvation. Now they are baby believers, like those I described earlier in the chapter. They're just waiting for direction on the next steps in their growth.

Here's my question: If Dave and Debbie are part of your church for the next several years, how do you want them to grow spiritually through your church's efforts? What do you want them to know and understand? To believe? To do? What are your expectations for Dave and Debbie to get involved in a ministry in your church? Assuming they grow in their faith over the next several years, what will that *look like* five years from now? How will your church help Dave and Debbie walk in that direction? One goal of this book is to answer the question of what every disciple of Christ ought to be, while also offering ideas for building a discipleship pathway in your church.

Why do these questions matter?

First, simply by asking these questions about your current and potential disciples, you will push your church toward determining discipleship goals.

Reflecting on years of working with congregations, church consultant Will Mancini notes that churches most often focus on *input* results (the "number of people and dollars that 'come into' the church"), rather than *output* results ("actual life-change outcomes that God intends for followers of Christ individually and together," including praying fervently, evangelizing well, and exhibiting the fruit of the Spirit).[13] In fact, some churches focus *only* on input results, talking about—even bragging about—metrics such as attendance and giving, without ever considering whether they are producing genuine disciples of Jesus. At the very least, determining and defining your church's "disciples" will shift your attention to *output* results.

Second, knowing who your disciples should be is only the first step in the process; your church must also establish a strategy for developing these disciples. It might be, however, that your church hasn't had an intentional discipling strategy for years, if not decades—or ever. As we've already noted, many churches simply carry out their programs the same way they've always done them— all the while assuming that participation will result in disciples. More likely, however, they will produce *faithful participants* who are not necessarily growing as disciples.

Aubrey Malphurs, a seminary professor and church consultant, reported years ago on a discipleship study that reached at least two conclusions: (1) "[church] leaders don't know what a disciple looks like," and (2) "they don't know how to make a disciple even if they can define one."[14] Far too often, church leaders have no defined goal in mind for discipleship; and even if they do have a goal, they have no strategy in place to achieve it. Envisioning what your disciples might look like down the road is insufficient if you don't have a plan to take them there. Even having a strategy on paper is not enough if you don't also have an action plan to accomplish it.

In my years as a church consultant, I have seen too many churches seek direction but not be willing to follow through with the necessary hard, intense work. They put together a strategy and then file it away because the work is too time-consuming and difficult. That can't happen if your church wants to produce disciples. My hope is that the rest of this book will help you at least get started in developing a strategy.

Third, knowing the characteristics of your potential disciples will help you set a growth goal and develop a discipleship plan to give to new members in your church.

Consider the following two scenarios from different churches.

In Church A, potential new members receive basic information about the church (for example, when I first joined a church many years ago, they gave me a Bible, a church constitution, and a box of offering envelopes). Newcomers learn about the church's history and vision, and they meet the pastoral staff. At the end of the class, they determine whether they're ready to officially join the church.

The membership class in Church B includes the same content, but their leaders intentionally spend significant time explaining to the attendees a plan of discipleship. They want new members to know (1) why the church believes that having a disciplemaking strategy is important, (2) what they want members to become as disciples, and (3) how they will help new members get there. In short, potential new members will hear, "We want you to be part of this church, but we also expect you to grow. And we've established a process to help you grow in Christ. We won't allow you to sit on the sidelines as a church member, but neither will we expect you to walk alone. We will help you become a disciple of Jesus who then disciples others."

Which of these churches would you rather join? My experience is that many people will choose to join churches that *expect something* from them and that have a plan to help them meet expectations. In fact, studies as far back as the 1970s have shown that congregations that expect more of their members tend to be growing churches.[15] People will join the ranks of a congregation whose faith is genuine, growing, and relevant.

Actually, that's another reason to make sure we are making disciples: Disciples who are growing in their faith attract other potential disciples. I know *I* would be attracted to a church committed to helping me grow toward maturity while also equipping me to make other disciples in the process.

Finally, consider this question: What do you do if Dave and Debbie are part of your church for many years but are never discipled? What is your church's plan to help longer-term, undiscipled believers begin growing for the first time? For that matter, what is your strategy to help faithful, growing believers *continue* to grow throughout their lives? No matter how long someone has been a believer, he or she should always be growing in Christ. Every disciple still needs discipling—and we must develop strategies for helping disciples grow at every stage of their Christian walk.

Quiz: Does Your Church Think They're Making Disciples?

It's time for another evaluation before we conclude this chapter. Third Church in the opening illustration of this chapter was a disciplemaking church, but First Church and Second Church would have also said they were making disciples. Most churches see themselves as disciplemakers at some level. Unfortunately, many churches that *think* they're disciplemaking churches really are not. Review each of the following statements that describe a particular type of church, and determine which type your church might be.[16]

1. **The church assumes it's a disciplemaking church because they affirm the Great Commission of Matthew 28:18-20, but they don't really make disciples.** Taking a biblical view or having a theologically accurate position does not always equate to disciplemaking. A theoretical commitment to making disciples without an accompanying plan doesn't accomplish much.

2. **The congregation is "doing church," but no one is measuring their disciplemaking results.** Even if they can show numerical growth in reaching nonbelievers, they don't evaluate the other side of the coin: How many of those new believers are learning to obey everything Jesus commanded (Matthew 28:20)?

3. **The church equates disciplemaking with programming.** That is, as previously noted, they assume you'll come out as a disciple of Christ if you participate in all their programs. Programs by themselves, however, don't make disciples. Disciples make disciples.

4. **The church has reduced disciplemaking to "information transfer."** The disciplemaking process in many churches amounts to little more than attending classes and gaining information. If you can answer the questions and talk the language, you're considered a disciple of Jesus.

5. **The church has several—if not many or most—leaders who themselves have never been strongly discipled.** They're more like Patrick in the introduction of this chapter than they are like growing disciples of Jesus. At best, they're trying to give others what they themselves have never received—and it's only remotely like biblical discipleship.

6. **The church offers a lot of activities, but with seemingly no strategic purpose.** These churches have a lot going on. They might even have a lot of people involved in their activities. However, they still cannot define a clear strategy for their process of disciplemaking.

7. **The church's disciplemaking approach (if any) tends not to be life-on-life.** A typical approach to discipleship is group oriented (e.g., worship service–based and small group–based) rather than individual (i.e., mentoring-based). Group approaches are necessary and helpful, but they don't always include much arm-in-arm, shoulder-to-shoulder encouragement and accountability between believers.

8. **The church encourages new members to get invested and involved, but they have no clear strategy to help them do that.** In many churches, it's not uncommon to find new(er) members who want to grow and be involved, but they've heard nothing about how to make that happen. That's often because the church has no plan.

9. **The church has numerous activities for kids and students, but no one is talking about coordinating those efforts to make young disciples of Christ.** Because most Christians become believers before they're eighteen, church youth ministries are missing an opportunity if they're not

thinking strategically.[17] Activities are good, but activities with a strategic purpose to make disciples are better.

10. **The church may do okay at raising up people to serve within their congregation, but they seldom send anyone out.** All their disciplemaking growth is internal, which can subtly become self-serving and self-preserving. New Testament disciples, however, give themselves up for the sake of others. They'll go to the ends of the earth if that is God's call on their lives.

EVALUATION FOR YOUR CHURCH
1. Would your members say they are a disciplemaking church?
2. What is your assessment of your church's disciplemaking efforts?

A Starting Point

Before we go any further, it's right to start where Jesus started when he made disciples: with the heart. Pastor Robby Gallaty puts it this way:

The discipleship process always begins here, with a personal relationship with Jesus. Before we embark on a journey to learn how to invest in the lives of others, we need to come back to this. The first step in learning isn't gathering information about models and methods. Jesus doesn't start by changing our actions—what we do. He first changes our *heart*.[18]

Discipleship begins with a fully committed follower of Christ who wants to raise up and equip others, with a goal of producing another generation of followers of Christ who commit to raising up successive generations. In other words, according to Gallaty, "Jesus expects us to be a disciple before we can be a maker of disciples."[19] Author Bill Hull, who has written much on discipleship, says the same thing in a slightly different way: "It is far more important to be a disciple than to have a plan to make disciples. When people are disciples, they will find a way to make other disciples. In fact, they won't be able to stop themselves."[20]

Again, this task begins with an examination of your own heart. Your church's discipleship can start to improve today if you personally strengthen your own commitment to Jesus. Are you walking faithfully with Christ? Is there an ongoing sin you need to confess? Do you need to give more attention to your spiritual disciplines? Have you made a commitment to invest in other, younger believers? Would those who know you best say you're a passionate and spiritually healthy follower of Jesus?

Wherever your heart is today, spend some time with the Lord before continuing this book. Then, let's continue the journey toward making disciples.

PERSONAL REFLECTION QUESTIONS

1. Which of the three stories in the opening section of this chapter best describes your own?
2. How would you define or describe a *disciple* of Jesus?
3. What one step can you take today to strengthen your church's disciplemaking?

CHAPTER 2

What Exactly Is a Disciple?

I HAVE BEEN a professor for more than twenty-five years, and it's tough to take the teacher out of me. So I naturally begin this chapter with a quiz question:

Q: Which of the following words or phrases defines a disciple of Jesus?

    A. Someone who obeys Jesus

    B. A follower of Jesus

    C. A student of Jesus

    D. Someone who reads her Bible and prays

    E. Someone who lives up to the name "Christian"

    F. All of the above

You would not be wrong if you chose any of the A–E options, but the best answer is F.

As we will see in this chapter, a disciple of Jesus is at least each of these things. I suspect most church members would get this question right, but I'm not convinced they think deeply about what it means personally to be a disciple of Jesus. I fear many church folks equate "disciple" with "church member" and give too little attention to their actual walk with Christ.

One goal of this chapter is to address the misconception that "church member" and "disciple" mean the same thing. More specifically, I want to help you and your church think about what a disciple *should be* according to the Scriptures. If you are going to determine the desired profile for disciples in your church, you want to start with a biblical foundation. So let's define our terms and press on together.

What Is Discipleship?

My friend and colleague Mark Liederbach defines discipleship as "the ongoing process of becoming and growing to be more like Christ and pursuing the mission we share with him for as long as we have life and being."[1] Discipleship is what followers of Christ are doing as they discipline their lives to obey Christ in order to become like him and "join Him on His mission with His other disciples."[2] Disciplemaking, then, is "a believer's intentional effort to invite, encourage, and equip others to become and grow to be more like Christ."[3]

I appreciate much about Mark's definitions. They recognize that *being* a disciple and *making* disciples are ongoing processes. Discipleship is much, much more than meeting with a mentor or attending a class; it is the sum of the believer's life. Further, the goal is to keep becoming more Christlike while also doing the work of the Great Commission (Matthew 28:18-20), as Jesus called us to do. We strive for these goals walking arm-in-arm with other believers, challenging each other to pursue and press in to God.

I think the best way to explain my own understanding of discipleship is to paint a word picture for you that encapsulates my definition of the term. Imagine a new convert who recently started following Christ. He is filled with zeal. His newfound faith is fresh, real, alive, and powerful. He'll talk about Jesus with anybody who will listen (and likely with some who don't want to listen). He's on fire for the Lord. In fact, he's more excited about his faith than many of the longtime members of his church.

You probably know what's likely to happen to him, however. Like Janie at First Church in the opening illustration of the last chapter, this new believer may lose his passion at some point. He might grow discouraged if others don't respond positively when he shares the gospel. Temptations may become overwhelming again. He may feel left out because he doesn't fit in with his old world anymore, but he also finds it hard to fit in with the church world. Then he looks around and sees many church members who don't seem to have much fire left. In fact, others with a continually burning fire in their hearts seem the exception rather than the rule, so this new believer eventually fades into the mediocrity that marks too many believers.

Have you seen similar things happen in your church? This all-too-common scenario raises a most significant question: How do we help believers *not* lose their fire and fall into this unhealthy pattern?

The answer? Walk beside them in a disciplemaking relationship so they can grow as disciples of Jesus. We walk beside each other to help keep the fire burning in all of us.

I define discipleship as the process of intentionally fueling the fire of Christ in a believer's life so that the fire doesn't go out. This process happens as individual believers choose to grow in Christlikeness *and* as other believers invest in them to encourage and equip them. Practicing spiritual disciplines—such as prayer, fasting, Bible study, service, confession, and worship, to name a few—is one means of fueling the fire, but so is learning from others as we practice spiritual disciplines together. Individually or corporately, we keep fueling the fire so our light will shine brightly in a dark world.

Growing disciples of Jesus have the fire of Christ burning in them as God conforms them to the image of his Son (Romans 8:29). What, then, does that look like?

Who Is a Disciple?

If you had asked me this question a few decades ago, I would have said that disciples primarily tell the gospel story to nonbelievers. That's because evangelism was my sole passion and my only training at that point in my spiritual journey. I thought that's what all followers of Jesus did. What I've learned since then is that being a disciple is not less than that, but it is surely more than that. Disciples live out the Great Commandment and the Great Commission, exhibit the fruit of the Spirit, wear the full armor of God, and obey Jesus.

A Disciple of Jesus Lives Out the "Two Greats"

In the previous chapter, I mentioned my gratitude to Rick Warren for his help in encouraging believers to make disciples through the local church. Warren is perhaps best known for his model of a healthy church based on the Great Commandment (Matthew 22:37-40) and the Great Commission (Matthew 28:19-20).[4] These two teachings describe what the church is supposed to be doing: worship ("love the LORD your God with all your heart"), ministry ("love your neighbor as yourself"), evangelism ("go and make disciples"), fellowship ("baptizing them"), and discipleship ("teaching them to obey").

Similar to Warren's understanding, Pastor J. T. English puts it this way:

> The Great Commission will be fulfilled by Great Commandment Christians. To be a Great Commandment Christian is to love God with your whole self and to love your neighbor. The Great Commission is to create Great Commandment Christians. The Great Commandment invites us to participate in the Great Commission, and the Great Commission invites us to participate in the Great Commandment.[5]

Disciples are to love God with all of their being, in every aspect of their lives. A disciple's commitment to God is to be so deep and so obvious that no one questions his or her commitment; it is life allegiance marked by willing and joyful obedience to whatever Jesus has commanded. This commitment is much more than the superficial, surface-level commitment that too many believers show today.

Moreover, disciples love their neighbors, who include not only their brothers and sisters in Christ but also their perceived enemies (Matthew 5:43-48; Luke 10:25-37). Disciples are to *be* neighbors who *love* neighbors—even the most unlovable ones—out of their overarching love for God. In fact, God's moving the hearts of believers to love their enemies has resulted in some of the most miraculous stories of healing and reconciliation I've experienced as a pastor. The overwhelming, transforming love of God has a way of granting us love for others that becomes a witness to the truth of the gospel.

That love for God and others is not only deep, but it's also broad enough to cover the world—because that's the love of God. In the words of pastor and scholar John Stott, "It seems to me legitimate to say that the love of Christ is 'broad' enough to encompass all mankind . . . , 'long' enough to last for eternity, 'deep' enough to reach the most degraded sinner, and 'high' enough to exalt him to heaven."[6] Disciples of Christ choose to play whatever role God has for them to get his message to the ends of the earth, and it is out of that love that they proclaim the gospel to all peoples of the world. Some go, and some support those who go, but all should have a heart to reach people. They evangelize nonbelievers, baptize new believers, and then teach them to obey Jesus—all under the power of Christ who promises to be with his followers "even to the end of the age" (Matthew 28:20).

Disciples, then, worship God, evangelize the lost, minister to others, live out their mission, and equip others—all as they grow in faith in the context of a local church family. To put it another way, disciples of Christ increasingly love God, love their neighbors, love the nations, and make disciples. The work of God in conforming them to the image of his Son (Romans 8:29) is evident in the way disciples grow internally, live faithfully, and witness widely.

When I think of people I know who have lived out the "Two Greats," I think of two in particular. My friend Shirley, a uniquely gifted sister in Christ, has given her life to serving others. I first met her when she was assisting in leading a single-adult group among our local Baptist churches in Ohio. Over the years, I've watched as she served singles around the world while her husband served in a US government role, led a ministry to teach teenage prison inmates in Texas, and generally encouraged her pastors along the way. Regardless of where she has been based, she has loved God and loved others.

My pastoral mentor, Tom Elliff, is the other person who comes to mind. Tom has served as a senior pastor, missionary, denominational leader, mission agency president, adjunct seminary professor, and itinerant speaker over the many years of his ministry—always with a spirit of humility. His love for God is evident. His commitment to evangelism, particularly among his neighbors, is convicting. His willingness to be a mentor and to be mentored even to this day (he's in his seventies) is encouraging. His desire to reach the nations for Christ is compelling. His passion for his family is always growing. When I speak with Tom, he sometimes talks about what the Lord is still teaching him. He is simply a man who wants to love God and others more.

That is not to suggest, however, that all believers will grow at the same rate as Shirley and Tom in living out the Great Commandment and the Great Commission. As Aubrey Malphurs reminds us, "The ultimate goal of the Great Commission is to produce mature believers. Once a person comes to faith, he or she begins the journey toward maturity. The reality is that all Christians are living at some point along the discipleship or maturity continuum. . . . Some are farther along and more committed than others."[7] Our responsibility is to reach believers where they are and guide them to live out the "Two Greats" as disciples of Christ. We get to walk with them as God makes all of us more like his Son.

Take a minute now to evaluate your church in light of the "Two Greats."

EVALUATION FOR YOUR CHURCH
1. Do your members increasingly love God with all their being? What evidence do you have for your assessment?
2. Do they love their neighbors and the nations?

A Disciple of Jesus Exhibits the Fruit of the Spirit

I memorized my first Bible verse when I attended youth Vacation Bible School for the first time at age fourteen. It was an easy verse—"God is love" (1 John 4:8)—but I needed an easy one to get started. After all, I hadn't even known before that Christians actually memorized the Bible! The next verses I memorized were a bit lengthier and included some words in the King James Version that were not in my vocabulary then: "But the fruit of the Spirit is love, joy, peace, longsuffering, gentleness, goodness, faith, meekness, temperance: against such there is no law" (Galatians 5:22-23, KJV). I think we sang a song that helped us remember these verses. It would be years, though, before I would understand the importance of bearing fruit in my life as a disciple of Christ.

Michael Wilkins, in his study of discipleship in the Gospel of John, concludes that disciples of Jesus will abide in his words, love other disciples, and bear fruit.[8] First, true disciples remain in God's Word. You can't miss that point if you listen to Jesus: "You are truly my disciples if you remain faithful to my teachings" (John 8:31).

As Colin Kruse observes in his commentary on John, "Jesus spoke of freedom from sin . . . and all it involves: freedom from condemnation (John 5:24), darkness (John 8:12), the power of the evil one (John 17:15; cf. 1 John 5:18), and death (John 5:24; 8:51)" when we obey him as his disciples.[9] We simply cannot separate our following of Jesus as his disciples from remaining in his Word and obeying his commands. Then again, why would we want to when obedience brings such freedom? We'll come back to this topic of obedience in a later section in this chapter.

Disciples also love one another, thus showing the first fruit of the Spirit in their lives (Galatians 5:22). That they must love other disciples seems almost obvious, given that disciples also love their enemies. Nevertheless, Jesus' words, "Love each other. Just

36

as I have loved you, you should love each other" (John 13:34) were radical enough that he preceded the words with, "So now I am giving you a new commandment." What was different was that they were to love one another *as Christ loved them*—with a profound, self-sacrificial love. They were to be brothers and sisters not only because they served together, but because they also shared the unifying love of God through Christ.

I could write all day about followers of Christ who've loved me through the years. On the day I became a believer, a lady I had never met said to me, "You don't know me, but I want you to know I love you. You're now my brother in Christ, and you're part of our family." To be honest, that was the first time I remember anyone telling me he or she loved me—and the words came from the lips of a disciple of Jesus who lived like Christ commanded. I am a better follower of Jesus today because I've heard those same words and sensed that same love from many other disciples since then.

Now we get to the primary point of this section: Disciples of Jesus must not only abide in God's Word and love one another, but they must also bear fruit: "Those who remain in me, and I in them, will produce much fruit. . . . When you produce much fruit, you are my true disciples" (John 15:5, 8). In fact, it is by their fruit that we can evaluate whether believers are truly following Christ as disciples (Matthew 7:20). Scholars debate what this "fruit" is—perhaps it's new converts, Christian character, Christlike love, missional living, increased faith, or a combination of things—but we know that fruit matters, as Galatians 5 tells us.

The apostle Paul compares life according to the flesh with life according to the Spirit. Those who follow Christ have been set free (Galatians 5:1), and it is by walking according to the Spirit that disciples maintain that victory. Indwelt by the Holy Spirit, their lives are marked by evidence of the Spirit's transforming power:

- love—the evidence of God, who is love, in one's life; the "source and fountain from which all of the other graces flow"[10]
- joy—rejoicing that is not dependent on circumstances; ongoing celebration of God's grace
- peace—harmony with God and others; not the absence of conflict or difficulty, but internal serenity that the world cannot comprehend (Philippians 4:7)
- patience—enduring faithfulness; forbearance without being easily frustrated or irritated
- kindness—affectionate care for others; offering good even to those who are undeserving; "benevolence in action"[11]
- goodness—generosity of spirit toward others; going "above and beyond"
- faithfulness—continually doing what we should as believers; loyalty to God and others; reliability
- gentleness—what the Bible sometimes calls *meekness*, a willing submission for the good of others; "strength under control"[12]
- self-control—the ability to resist the temptations of the enemy; not indulging the flesh

All believers should exhibit the fruit of the Spirit because the Spirit resides in each believer. Just like an apple tree produces apples, followers of Christ should produce fruit that models Christ. "In an ultimate sense," says scholar Donald K. Campbell, "this 'fruit' is simply the life of Christ lived out in a Christian."[13]

At the same time, though, we believers must strive together to help each other cultivate this fruit by living the Christian life. God created us to need each other (1 Corinthians 12:12-27), and no one is designed to grow on their own. We are disciples who

make disciples as we encourage one another to exhibit the fruit
of the Spirit.

EVALUATION FOR YOUR CHURCH
1. How much attention has your church given to teaching
   about the fruit of the Spirit?
2. What is your church's process for evaluating whether
   members exhibit the fruit of the Spirit?

A Disciple of Jesus Wears the Full Armor of God

I started studying the reality of spiritual warfare many years ago,
when, frankly, I was trying to learn to love my earthly father. He
became a believer at age seventy-one, and the final three years of
his life were special ones as he lived out his nascent faith—but I
struggled prior to that point to love him as a Christian should. It
was while I was reading Ephesians 6 one day, though, that things
really began to change.[14]

I had read the text before, but on this day, God focused my
attention on these words: "We are not fighting against flesh-and-
blood enemies, but against evil rulers and authorities of the unseen
world, against mighty powers in this dark world, and against evil
spirits in the heavenly places" (Ephesians 6:12). For the first time, I
saw clearly that my dad was not my enemy, regardless of what had
happened in the past. I was instead facing a supernatural enemy
holding my dad in spiritual bondage and seeking to hold me in
bondage to bitterness and anger. It was in that context that I began
to consider what it means to wear "the full armor of God" that Paul
describes in Ephesians 6.

To understand what the armor is and how it works, we need
to know how Ephesians 6:10-17 fits into the wider book of

Ephesians.[15] Why Paul wrote this epistle is not entirely clear. Most likely, it was a circular letter designed to instruct and encourage believers throughout the region of Asia Minor. What *is* clear about the book, however, is its structure. The first three chapters are theological in nature, and the final three chapters are practical.

In particular, the first chapters emphasize the *position* of believers in Christ. They resound with phrases describing God's work in us. We are "saints *in Christ Jesus*" (Ephesians 1:1, CSB, with italics added here and below) whom God has blessed with every blessing "in the heavens *in Christ*" (1:3). He "chose us *in him*" (1:4), "adopted [us] as sons" *through him* (1:5), and lavished grace on us "*in the Beloved One*" (1:6). We are told that "*in him* we have redemption through his blood" (1:7), have "received an inheritance" (1:11), and have been "sealed with the promised Holy Spirit" (1:13).

Moreover, God has "made us alive *with Christ*" (Ephesians 2:5). He has "raised us up *with him* and seated us *with him* in the heavens *in Christ Jesus*" (2:6), ever extending his "kindness to us *in Christ Jesus*" (2:7). He has also created us for good works "*in Christ Jesus*" (2:10). In him we who were once "far away" from God have also been "brought near" (2:13). We have access to the Father through him (2:18), and it is in him that the church exists in unity. Put all of this together and it's clear why "*in him* we have boldness and confident access through faith *in him*" (3:12). In good discipleship, by the way, we have the privilege of helping believers know who they are in Christ too.

The final three chapters of Ephesians build on the first three, with Paul appealing to believers to "walk worthy of the calling you have received" (4:1). In fact, Paul emphasizes living out our faith in every area of our lives: in our personal walk, in our family, in our church, and in our workplace.[16] We believers who are disciples of Jesus are to *walk*—that is, to conduct ourselves—differently than the world does:

- "Walk worthy of the calling you have received" (Ephesians 4:1, CSB).
- "You should no longer walk as the Gentiles do, in the futility of their thoughts" (Ephesians 4:17, CSB).
- "Walk in love, as Christ also loved us and gave himself for us" (Ephesians 5:2, CSB).
- "Walk as children of light—for the fruit of the light consists of all goodness, righteousness, and truth" (Ephesians 5:8-9, CSB).
- "Pay careful attention, then, to how you walk—not as unwise people but as wise" (Ephesians 5:15, CSB).

How do we get there? God gives us pastors and teachers who model Christian living, shepherd us, and equip us "for the work of ministry" (Ephesians 4:12, CSB). They ground us in biblical truth by teaching the Word, show us faithfulness through godly living, and challenge us to be disciples by personal disciplemaking. Our pastors help prepare us for the battle we all face against the evil principalities and powers of the spirit world (Ephesians 6:12).

God also graciously gives us other believers who model Christian growth for us and challenge us in that direction. Each believer may have a different role in the church (1 Corinthians 12), but all are part of the body of Christ. The church, then, is not a building in which we gather; it is who we are as brothers and sisters in Christ. We are disciples raising up other disciples.

Paul ends his letter to the Ephesians with a call for believers to "put on the full armor of God" (Ephesians 6:11, CSB; cf. 6:13).

That passage, designed to leave the reader with a memorable summary of the letter and a final challenge, is not some mystical call simply to "pray on" the armor of God; rather, it is a call to live faithfully as disciples of Christ. Each piece of the armor builds on our position in Christ and calls us to live out our faith practically.[17]

Think about the armor in light of being a disciple of Christ. Wearing the belt of truth means knowing Jesus, who is truth (John 14:6), *and* living as a person of truth. Wearing the breastplate of righteousness means faithfully living out the righteousness God gives us (Philippians 3:9). Thus, wearing the belt and breastplate rules out hypocrisy in a genuine disciple of Christ.

Wearing the shoes reflects our proclaiming the gospel of peace—the story of God's reconciling us to himself through Christ. Carrying the shield of faith means trusting the promises of Christ, who is the "champion who initiates and perfects our faith" (Hebrews 12:2). To wear the helmet of salvation is to live out God's grace, always pointing to Christ, who is our salvation. It is to give evidence of the new nature God has created in us (Ephesians 4:24). Finally, to take up the sword of the Spirit is to follow Christ—who is the Word (John 1:1-5)—and to live and proclaim his Word.

What, then, does wearing the full armor of God mean for us as we consider discipleship? First, discipleship requires teaching and learning the Word of God. Not only does Paul ground the entire book of Ephesians in theology, but every piece of the armor is somehow connected to the Word. The Word is truth, and it is in the Word that we learn about righteousness. Scripture reveals the gospel of peace to us. Carrying the shield of faith is directly connected to our hearing the Word (Romans 10:17). And, of course, it is the Word that teaches us about the salvation God has given us.

We simply cannot be strong disciples apart from knowing, following, and teaching the Word. A true disciple of Jesus will faithfully remain in his Word.

Second, discipleship requires our teaching other believers to live out their position in Christ. How do we best help new believers to keep their fire burning? We teach them the Word. We show them how to walk in truth and righteousness. We model for them a method of sharing the gospel. We teach them—and, just as important, show them—how to trust God in faith. We also help them read, understand, and apply the Word as they live out their salvation and lead others to do the same.

If we don't teach disciples how to wear the armor, we cannot be surprised when they lose battle after battle. Without discipleship, believers are hardly ready for the war we're all in. On the other hand, we defeat the enemy and his forces not by some unique warfare approach, but by fundamental obedience to Christ. Fully following Jesus means warding off the enemy's arrows as we walk in righteousness, trust his promises, and proclaim his message. A fire that keeps burning is a fire that threatens the enemy—and discipleship helps keep the fire aglow.

EVALUATION FOR YOUR CHURCH
1. How much attention has your church given to teaching about the armor of God?
2. What evidence is there that some of your church's members have never been discipled?

A Disciple of Jesus Obeys Him

In some ways, we've already made this point. A follower of Jesus who lives out the "Two Greats," who exhibits the fruit of the Spirit, and who wears the full armor of God will be walking in *obedience* to Christ. I emphasize obedience here because Jesus is so clear about what he expects from his followers: "If you love me, obey my commandments" (John 14:15). Those who accept Christ's commands *and* obey them are those who love him (John 14:21). All who love him will do what he says (John 14:23). Believers are his friends if they do what he commands (John 15:14).

Loving God simply means keeping his commandments (1 John 5:3). Conversely, those who don't love Jesus will not keep his words (John 14:24). Gerald Borchert, one of my former professors, summarizes what this obedience means: "Obeying Jesus' commands in effect means to copy the example of Jesus."[18] Disciples are to be like Christ.

When I was a young believer, a friend gave me a copy of Charles M. Sheldon's book *In His Steps*.[19] First published in 1896 (long before the WWJD? bracelet craze), Sheldon's book is a fictional story of a congregation challenged by their pastor to ask the question, "What would Jesus do?" before doing anything for one year. As you might expect, asking that question led to changed lives among the members of that congregation.

I confess that I read the book as a young believer without anyone to guide me in its application. I took the message to heart, but I turned it into legalism and arrogance. I not only asked the question for myself, but I also pointed out to others when they needed to live more like Jesus. Looking back, I know I lived less like Jesus some days after trying to apply that book in my life. I also think about how I might have lived differently if I'd had a mentor to point out the errors in my life—to help me see myself with disciplemaking eyes.

Nevertheless, the question the book raises is an important one that lays out a powerful challenge for disciples of Jesus. To follow him is to imitate him—to "copy the example of Jesus," in Dr. Borchert's words.

The apostle Paul not only understood this calling, but he also recognized the significance of his modeling Christ for others. He urged believers to imitate him (1 Corinthians 4:16; 11:1; Philippians 3:17; 1 Thessalonians 1:6; 2 Thessalonians 3:7), and he connected their imitation of him to his personal walk with Jesus.

Confident in the work of the Holy Spirit in his life, Paul could write to the Corinthians, "You should imitate me, just as I imitate Christ" (1 Corinthians 11:1). Paul, the Corinthians' father in the faith, modeled that faith before them and challenged them to live for Christ as he did. As one scholar said about the Corinthians, they "had not seen Jesus in the flesh: they had no Bible; but they had seen Paul"[20]—and that relationship directed them to Christ.

Earlier, I mentioned my dad. When my dad became a believer, God dramatically transformed him in ways we could never have imagined. His temper became patience. His growl became a smile. He read the Bible for the first time in his seventies and devoured the Word as much as his diabetes-affected eyes would let him. When he passed away, I was privileged to speak at his funeral. To prepare, I spent some time thinking about ways I'm like he was even though our relationship was not always the strongest.

I am right-handed, but I shoot a gun and play pool left-handed because my left-handed dad taught me how to do both activities. I tie my shoes like a lefty for the same reason. When I'm engrossed in a task (such as writing this book), my tongue protrudes just slightly from my lips—exactly like my dad's did when he was focused. I'm over sixty years old, but I still field a baseball like my dad taught me: charging the ball, keeping both my gloved hand and my free hand on the ground, keeping my eye on the ball, blocking it if necessary with my body. I can still see my dad showing me what to do, and I can hear his voice of instruction echoing in my head. To this day, I imitate him in ways I don't even recognize.

How much more important it is for disciples to emulate Jesus! Only when others see Christ in his disciples will they see the authenticity and power that will attract them to the Lord. Genuine disciples of Christ who live fully for him will point others to him. In fact, every believer reading this book must model Jesus for others. We who are shepherds in God's church are particularly responsible for being an example to the flock (1 Peter 5:3). Making disciples ourselves is one way of modeling Jesus, as the next chapter will show.

EVALUATION FOR YOUR CHURCH
1. Does your church challenge members to live in such a way that to imitate them would be to imitate Christ?
2. Does your church have any process for encouraging wandering believers to start living like Jesus again?

The Dust of the Teacher

Who is a disciple of Jesus? The believer who lives out the "Two Greats," exhibits the fruit of the Spirit, wears the full armor of God, and imitates Christ through obedience. That's the kind of Christ-followers we are all meant to be.

In my seminary office, I have a picture of myself with Brandon—a man I mentored—and his son, Samuel. In the completely candid photo, the three of us are walking together across a seminary yard—with me in front, followed by Brandon and then Samuel. Written across this photo of three generations of

Christ-followers are the words, "The disciple walks in the dust of the teacher."[21] Those words paint a picture that continually forces me to examine myself—to ask whether I want other believers to walk in my dust.

Am I a devoted disciple of Christ? As a follower of Jesus, am I living out the Great Commandment and the Great Commission? Does my life give evidence of the fruit of the Spirit residing in me? Am I wearing the full armor of God, confirmed by my walking in truth and righteousness? Am I walking with Christ in such a way that I would be comfortable with others imitating my life?

Moreover, I must ask, "Am I multiplying disciples by investing in others?" and "Is my church truly a disciplemaking church?" I pray this chapter prompts you and your congregation to ask these same questions.

PERSONAL REFLECTION QUESTIONS

1. At this point in the book, how has your definition of *disciple* changed, if at all?
2. Of the four areas that describe a disciple—living out the "Two Greats," exhibiting the fruit of the Spirit, wearing the full armor of God, obeying Christ—where are you strongest? Weakest?
3. Who in your life most imitates Christ? Who in your life is most likely watching whether *you* imitate Christ?

CHAPTER 3

Getting Started as a Disciplemaking Church

START SOMEWHERE. Do something.

That's the refrain I want you to hear as you read this chapter. If you want your church to be a disciplemaking church, you must start somewhere. You must do something.

Some years ago, I was struggling with a difficult career decision. I had two options on the table—both which would have been good, and both of interest to me. I prayed and sought advice, but still I wrestled day and night with the decision. Looking back, I'm certain I wouldn't have gone wrong with either one. At the time, though, I kept delaying my answer in hopes I would get clear direction from the Lord.

Here's what happened: Because I took so much time to make my decision, both options disappeared. Both potential employers viewed my delay as a lack of commitment and enthusiasm for the job, and they withdrew their offers. I fully understand that decision now, and I likely would have done the same thing if I were in their shoes. A failure to act on an opportunity before us usually says something about us.

What's my point? As you begin taking steps to strengthen your church's disciplemaking, don't get so bogged down in the work of developing a process that you don't actually *do* something. In some churches, the steps needed to develop a good disciplemaking strategy could take many months, if not years. If too many committees and teams have to give their input, the process itself could drain leadership of their early enthusiasm, and the plans may ultimately be shelved. But if I've described your church here, this doesn't have to be your story.

As we faithfully follow God in making disciples, every one of us must heed the challenge laid down by pastor and author Kevin DeYoung: "*Just do something!*"[1] The goal of this chapter is to help you take some steps in the right direction. I have listed these beginning steps somewhat sequentially, but you must determine which ones best fit your church's context. In any case, you must do *something* toward making disciples through your church. The next chapter will add further ideas for implementation, but let's begin at the starting line.

Determine Your Own Commitment to Discipleship

In a previous book in this Church Answers series, *The Potential and Power of Prayer*, I wrote about the influence of pastors in a local church, with particular reference to the Great Commission and prayer.[2] Never in my years of doing ministry and studying churches have I seen Great Commission–minded or prayerful churches without a pastor whose passions are the same. No church I've known has these heartbeats without a pastor who leads the way. I would say the same about strong disciplemaking churches.

Indeed, discipleship leader Greg Ogden drives home the point: "If a church is going to become a disciple-making congregation and build a culture of discipleship, it must be the lifestyle of the core leadership, starting with the senior or lead pastor."[3] The shadow of any leader falls long on an organization, and that's particularly true in a local church.

The problem is that some leaders who talk about discipleship are neither prepared for nor committed to the work that must be done. In some cases, the leaders themselves have never really been discipled. If that's your situation, take heart. You are not alone.[4] Over the years, I've met far more undiscipled people than discipled ones, including many church leaders. I sense that pattern is changing, but it still leaves many leaders longing for help and growth.

God wants all followers of Christ—and especially leaders—to move past the milk of the Word to get to the meat (Hebrews 5:11-14). God is glorified as he transforms us to be more like Jesus and as he uses mature believers to show others the way. He wants us to be growing in Christlikeness, and that requires honest confession and intentional discipleship. There's nothing wrong with being honest about where you are on your journey if you've never been discipled; in fact, it's the right thing to do.

If you're honest about your need, trust that God will provide someone to disciple you—an apostle Paul for your life. God did not design you to carry your ministry responsibilities and burdens alone, and he will create what I call "divine intersections" to put a disciplemaker in your life.[5] When we genuinely seek to grow in our relationship with God, he connects us with others. My prayer for you is that God will work so strongly in your life through someone else that others will take note. I want others to say, "God's up to something in my church leader's life!"

If you're committed to discipleship but are still looking for a Paul in your life, here are some suggestions to help you find that person:

1. **Pray for a mentor.** God alone crisscrosses lives in such a way that both lives are strengthened. Ask him to reveal those intersections in your life.

2. **Look around.** Pay attention to believers whose lives you trust. Look for those whose walk with God you want to emulate. Pray about asking one of those people to disciple you.

3. **Ask . . . and keep asking until you find someone to disciple you.** Consider asking someone near you *or* someone who might be available only via electronic means. Don't stop looking and asking until you find somebody.

4. **Be grateful for whatever another believer might offer.** Even if your potential disciplemaker cannot give you all you want, be thankful for what you get. One hour with the right mentor is worth weeks of waiting for the next meeting.

5. **Invest in somebody else yourself.** Even while you are seeking someone to disciple you, you may have something you can teach somebody else. You might find that God will direct you to a discipler *after* you begin discipling others.[6] (We will come back to this suggestion later in the chapter.)

As we've noted, some church leaders are ill-prepared to lead in disciplemaking because no one's ever discipled them. Other leaders may have been discipled at some point, but they have very little passion for or commitment to the work of discipleship. They expect church members to make disciples, but they're not discipling anyone themselves. They emphasize participation in small groups even while they're not attending one. They push life-on-life discipleship but have no mentor investing in them; they're walking their path alone while expecting church members to do something different. Pastors and small group facilitators promote discipleship from the pulpit and within their groups, but they leave discipleship at the "information transfer" level when they fail to help believers *apply* biblical truth through their teaching. Their heart is simply not in the task of disciplemaking, regardless of what they might say.

Mature disciplemakers are simply different. They *do* what they challenge others to do even as they equip them. In describing a church's shift from *informing* people to *equipping* them, Jim Putman, senior pastor of Real Life Ministries in Idaho, concludes, "It starts with honest, humble leaders who are living out in their personal relationships what they want other people to live out in theirs."[7] Disciplemaking leaders model godly living for others as they imitate Christ.

These leaders must also raise up others to do the work of ministry; that is, they are intentionally not the center of the show. In the words of Jim Putman, "A leader's job is to guide and equip the saints so that the entire church becomes a mature community in which disciples flourish. It involves releasing the ministry and gifts of all believers. It's about creating a place where everybody learns to be a minister by growing, serving, and making disciples themselves."[8]

Let's do some personal evaluation. Using these questions, evaluate your own commitment to discipleship:

- If you are a church leader, are you the kind of reproducing leader Putman describes?
- Do you have a mentor who pushes you to continue to grow in Christ?
- Are you personally participating in one of your church's small groups?
- Are you discipling anyone with purpose and direction?
- If you are a teacher or preacher, do you work hard at teaching not only content but also application of that content?
- Do you prioritize discipleship in your calendar?
- Would those who know you best say that discipleship is genuinely important to you?

I assume you want to strengthen discipleship in your church, or you would have put this book down by now. As we've done before, start with yourself. If you know you need to take steps to be a better disciple as an example to your church, I encourage you to make that commitment now. In fact, write that commitment here, including noting the biggest obstacle you'll need to overcome to accomplish it. Be sure, then, to share it with someone in your church. Hold yourself accountable as part of your own discipleship.

"My commitment is _____

_____."

"The biggest obstacle I will face to keeping this commitment
is _____."

"My plan to overcome that obstacle is _____
_____."

Enlist a Discipleship Prayer Team

Much has been written about shifts we need to make in our
churches if we want to become disciplemaking congregations.
Jim Putman, for example, argues for shifts from reaching people
to making disciples; from informing people to equipping them;
from program-based discipleship to purposeful, hands-on training; from activities to relationships; and from accumulating members to deploying them.[9] Greg Ogden similarly emphasizes the
need for churches to "shift from an emphasis on making disciples
through programs to making disciples through relationships."[10]
J. T. English rightly calls the church to shift in the questions we
ask—for example, from "What do disciples want?" to "What
do disciples need?" and from "How do we keep disciples in the
church?" to "How do disciples grow in the church?"[11]

All these proposed shifts are on target, but I want to add
another important one. We need to shift from a "plan first, pray
second" mode to a "pray first, plan second" mode. Too often, our
churches operate in plan-first mode, even though we know better.
We may pray a perfunctory prayer as we plan, but let's be honest: Much of the time, we plan first and ask God to honor what
we've already planned. Then we wonder with surprise why our
plans don't always work out. We simply cannot assume that an
unprayed-for discipleship strategy will accomplish much. Indeed,
as professors John Mark Terry and J. D. Payne have said, "If
strategy is from the Lord, then prayer is a part of the process of

knowing, understanding, and accomplishing what the Father has in mind in making disciples of the people."[12]

The words of the great English preacher Charles Spurgeon are especially convicting to me here:

> Prayer must always be the fore horse of the team. Do whatever else is wise, but not until thou hast prayed. Send for the physician if thou art sick; but first pray. Take the medicine if thou hast a belief that it will do thee good; but first pray. Go and talk to the man who has slandered you, if you think you ought to do so; but first pray. "Well, I am going to do so and so," says one, "and I shall pray for a blessing on it afterwards." Do not begin it until you have prayed. Begin, continue, and end everything with prayer; but especially begin with prayer.[13]

If you are seeking to strengthen your church's discipleship strategy, seek God first. Enlist a group of three to five believers who represent the makeup of your church, and ask God to grant you collective wisdom and insight. Ask the group to pray for your walk with God as you lead others to assess their own lives. In my book *Discipled Warriors*, I challenge churches to enlist a standing prayer team for each of the six purposes of the church: worship, evangelism, equipping/discipling, ministry, prayer, and fellowship.[14] How might our churches change if faithful believers were to cover in prayer everything we did? What would happen if we *began*, *continued*, and *ended* everything with prayer?

Several reasons for developing this prayer team come to mind. First, we are talking about helping others become more like Christ—so why would we not seek Christ first on behalf of others? After all, none of us has the ability or the giftedness to be disciples or to create disciples on our own. Without the help of the one to whom we pray, few things will change for the better in our disciplemaking. We need "dependence on prayer rather than a program for prayer."[15]

Second, revitalizing a discipling process (or starting one) usually requires an admission of our past and present failures in this regard. Jim Collins's bestseller, *Good to Great*, relates to businesses rather than churches, but his point that leaders must "confront the brutal facts (yet never lose faith)" to improve their organizations is on target for churches, too.[16] Confronting the brutal facts in a church with poor discipleship, however, might mean addressing leaders we should never have appointed in the first place; challenging a small group leader to strengthen his or her own quiet time; tightening the criteria by which a church selects deacons; calling members to holiness with more pointedness than they've heard before; or even carrying out church discipline when necessary to call believers to repentance. As we ramp up our commitment to biblical discipleship, prayer cannot be optional if we want to deal with the realities of what it takes to grow in our faith.

Third, we can rest assured that the enemy will oppose our efforts to help church members put on the full armor of God (Ephesians 6:10-17). Satan is ruthless, seeking to devour baby believers before they ever get started. He is vindictive, aiming to tear down longtime believers and undermine their witness. He targets pastors who commit to disciplemaking, congregations that grow in this desire, and individuals who seek discipling. Given the wicked, divisive intentions of Satan and his forces, it's no wonder Paul concludes the armor of God passage with this mandate for believers: "Pray in the Spirit at all times and on every occasion. Stay alert and be persistent in your prayers for all believers everywhere" (Ephesians 6:18). Disciplemaking churches must be churches that pray with urgency.

Establishing an ongoing prayer team that focuses on discipleship is also an opportunity to develop disciples of Jesus. Teaching members of the team to pray with focus and insight may also strengthen their personal and family prayer times. Plus, when leaders remind the congregation how much prayer has gone into their discipleship efforts, it sends a signal that spiritual formation and growth are significant priorities for the church. Build your discipleship prayer team quickly. You will not regret it.

Take a few minutes now to evaluate your church in this light.

EVALUATION FOR YOUR CHURCH
1. On a scale of 1 to 10 (with 1 being the lowest), how committed to prayer is your church?
2. How much attention has your congregation given in the past to praying over their disciplemaking efforts?

Celebrate Progress

As I've been writing, I've spent a lot of time thinking about my own discipleship journey as a follower of Christ. I've tried to encapsulate it in five phases, from my forty-five-plus years of following Christ. As you read my description of each stage, think about your own journey. Pay attention to the times of progress in your spiritual walk, and celebrate the Lord's work in you.

Phase 1: *"I can't believe God has saved me and made me his child."* In those earliest days, the gospel was so real that my fire for Christ just exploded. Indeed, I suspect I was an obnoxious new believer. Every positive step, though, was progress.

Phase 2: *"It's cool to teach others the Bible."* I was a teenage teacher in a kids Vacation Bible School class at the time, but it didn't matter what the context was. Even as a fairly new believer who hadn't been discipled well, I enjoyed teaching God's Word. Under God's grace, I was moving in the right direction.

Phase 3: *"I'm kind of proud of who I am."* I started pastoring full-time at age twenty. Our denomination even recognized my first church for its outreach—which made me think I must be ahead of others. Later, I pastored one of the larger churches in the area. In my youthful arrogance and zeal, I was sure I had "arrived." The progress in my walk slowed at best.

Phase 4: *"Wow. Ministry's really hard and humbling."* My prideful heart began to change a bit as the day-to-day grind of ministry sliced some layers off my ego. Serving as a spiritual leader in a local church has a way of reminding you how much you need God. Remembering that truth was progress again.

Phase 5: *"More than ever before, I can't believe God has saved me."* Decades of following Christ have brought me back to seeing my sin again and again, and appreciating God's grace even more. I cannot fathom why God has chosen to use me, warts and all. The older I get, the more I realize how much I still need to grow—and the more I celebrate what God is doing in me.

As long as God gives me life, I'll still be learning how to be Christlike. I won't fully get there while I'm here on earth. What I'm learning more and more is that we never outgrow our need to grow—and that's an okay position to be in. You will always need someone to stoke your fire for Christ by discipling you. Robert Coleman's words challenge me again:

I've lived long enough to realize how little I know, but I yearn to grasp so much more when I have a Teacher who can answer my questions. So the future is exciting. . . . When we step over the line and decide to follow Jesus and embrace the discipleship lifestyle, we become lifelong learners. I suspect this will go on forever.[17]

Daniel Im is right when he says that discipleship is not about arriving at a destination as much as it is about moving in the right direction; it is recognizing that spiritual maturity is "an ongoing process without an endpoint this side of eternity."[18] We press forward "to reach the end of the race" (Philippians 3:14), and we press on together in the context of discipleship relationships. When we make this commitment, we will keep striving to grow as disciples and as disciplemakers.

What does this ongoing process mean for us as disciplemakers? It means we never stop growing, our work is never fully finished in this world, and we must be okay with works in progress. Even for those of us who like to check off completed projects, *incompleteness* will be a reality of the discipleship process until the Lord calls us home. Baby believers need us to teach them how to feed themselves spiritually even as we continue to learn to feed ourselves. And we celebrate as God grows us.

It also means that we must be patient with those we disciple. Their trajectory in following Jesus may be like a car on a roller coaster: up and down, fast and slow, around in circles. But even a roller coaster is headed in the right direction to the right place, and it will eventually get there. Our disciples, I trust, are typically moving in the right direction, even if it takes them a while to get where they're going. We need to celebrate progress and continue to trust God to grow them toward maturity.

Because we, too, must continue to grow, we must model for others what it means to be continually growing in Christ. Another one of my spiritual heroes (whom I'll refer to as TB for security reasons) has followed the Lord for many decades. He is a missionary who has served in some of the riskiest places on earth. He has also served as a pastor and denominational leader. TB is a prolific reader, and he has continued his formal education into his sixties. When he and I talk, it's not uncommon for him to tell me what he has been learning lately through God's Word. TB is a role model for me, but he'll tell you he's just a fellow traveler learning how to follow Jesus. He is a disciple of Christ still moving in the right direction. That's what matters—and that's progress worth celebrating.

Begin Investing in Two or Three Others

I run almost every day. I'm sure some trainers would tell me to take some days off, but I know myself well. If I take off one day, that one day easily becomes two . . . and three . . . and before I know it, I'm out of shape again. For me, consistency is key.

Over the years, however, I have never run an official race. I'm not sure why I haven't. I'm as competitive as anyone I know. I look forward to a challenge. I have enough ego that I like "holding my own" against younger competitors. It makes sense that I would plan to run a race, perhaps one like the 5K race our seminary sponsors for missions. I just haven't done it.

Here's what I know, though. Any plans I make to run a race will mean nothing until I step up to the starting line, hear the starter gun go off, and begin running. Unless I start somewhere, I won't get anywhere. It's the same when it comes to developing a discipleship strategy in a church: If you don't start *somewhere*, it will never happen. In my judgment, the place to start is by investing in two or three other believers—to begin mentoring others—even as you're leading your church to develop a disciplemaking process.

You might remember my definition of discipleship as "the process of intentionally fueling the fire of Christ in a believer's life so the fire doesn't go out." My definition of mentoring is similar, but more narrowly focused. As I've written elsewhere, mentoring is "a God-given relationship in which one growing Christian encourages and equips another believer to reach his or her potential as a disciple of Christ."[19] On the one hand, discipleship is a broad category that can include large group, small group, or one-on-one components; it is the entirety of what the church does to move believers in the direction of Christian maturity. Mentoring, then, is the most personal component of discipleship. To put it another way, mentoring is part of discipleship, but discipleship includes more than just mentoring.

Why does mentoring matter in your church's discipleship plan? The answer is simple: because it allows us to be "iron sharpening iron" (see Proverbs 27:17) in our discipling relationships. When we have relationships with others who push us toward maturity, we help each other become more Christlike. Thus, the moment you start mentoring someone, you will have begun strengthening your church's disciplemaking process even as you're still working on the larger discipleship approach for your congregation. Even one disciple making another disciple will strengthen the entire church.

Your responsibility is to lead the way, so start the race by mentoring two or three other believers.

Howard Hendricks, a longtime seminary professor, defined "three kinds of mentoring relationships that [every believer] desperately needs to pursue,"[20] which he illustrated with three people from the New Testament. First, he said, we all need a Paul, an older believer who can build into our life. Next, we need a Barnabas, a close friend and peer, to whom we can be account-able. Finally, we all need a Timothy, a younger believer into whose life we are building.[21] To this list, I would add a fourth relation-ship that all believers need: a friendship with a nonbeliever with whom we're sharing the gospel. That way, we keep our eyes turned outward toward the lost even as we are growing with fellow believ-ers. And that nonbeliever friend could become another Timothy in your life.

If you don't already have these people in your life, do what Dr. Hendricks often invited others to do: Ask God to lead you to a Paul, a Barnabas, and a Timothy—and, if you follow my sugges-tion, to a nonbeliever. Be patient as God brings people into your life in his own timing, but always be alert for opportunities. Don't miss a chance for growth because you weren't looking for it.

Our particular focus in this section is on finding a Timothy. Ultimately, we want to have all four types of relationships, but a Timothy might be the easiest one to find at first. Begin by asking God to direct you to a younger believer to invest in. Jesus prayed (all night long, actually) before he called his twelve apostles (Luke 6:12-13). We would be wise to follow his example. If we don't pray about our choices, we're likely to pick someone who is most like us—and that may not be God's plan. He might surprise you by his choice of a Timothy.

As you're praying for God's direction, begin to look for indi-viduals who seem inquisitive, or who seek you out for advice, or who give evidence of a desire to grow spiritually. Some have sug-gested identifying people who are faithful, available, and teachable (perhaps you've seen the acronym FAT).[22] I don't disagree with that direction, but we want to be certain we have sought God's direc-tion before choosing someone to mentor. If we're following God's leading, it may be that a person who doesn't always follow through, is often busy, and initially resists our input will change dramatically under the influence of our mentoring. Remember, discipleship means moving a person *in the direction of* Christian maturity.

My guess is that there are people in your life already who are potential mentees, but you may not have been thinking about them that way. Notice who hangs out with you after the worship service at church. Look around your small group for enthusiastic members. Meet some newer believers at a coffee shop. If you're a pastor, you might have lunch with another staff member just to get caught up—and see whether the Lord might be directing you to a mentoring relationship together. Prayerfully find *somebody* to invest in.

Next, set your goals high for the people you're discipling. Begin to pray now that God will use these believers in even greater ways than he's used you. Trust that the witness and work of the next generations of Christ followers will far exceed yours—and urge them in that direction. Your church will be stronger tomorrow if you will invest in someone today.

One of the fun facts in my life is that the provost of the seminary where I teach is one of my former students from twenty-plus years ago. I mentored him back then, and now he leads me today. When I first had a meal with him decades ago, neither of us would have dreamed that I would one day report to him. That's what happened, though—and I could not be more thrilled. I love how the Lord is using him! As you look for believers to mentor, ask God to give you a big vision for how he might use those you disciple.

At the same time, don't worry about developing a mentoring plan up front. Making disciples through mentoring is not a project; it's the privilege of being in a God-centered discipling relationship. The needs of your mentees will differ, and how you mentor each one will vary. Spend time together and let the relationship guide you in developing your strategy.

In my book *Mentor*, I encourage a "goal-oriented informality" in mentoring relationships that has intentionality in purpose but freedom in process.[23] You will have some sense of what you want to accomplish with your mentee, but be open to adjusting as you learn more about each other. You might begin with weekly, monthly, or twice-a-month meals together. Ask a lot of questions. Learn all you can about your mentee's walk with God. Seek the Lord together, and then decide your next steps.

You might have also noticed that I'm suggesting you invest in two or three others instead of only one. I'd rather see you pour yourself into one person than none, but I prefer that leaders broaden their influence to a few more, if possible. Jesus clearly spent more time with Peter, James, and John than with the other disciples, and we might assume that all the disciples learned from each other as well as from Jesus. Your mentees can do the same if you plan time for the three or four of you to meet together and "motivate one another to acts of love and good works" (Hebrews 10:24).

So start somewhere. Do something.

EVALUATION FOR YOUR CHURCH

1. If you're a leader in your church (and therefore an example to others), who is your Paul? Your Barnabas? Your Timothy? Your nonbeliever?
2. How much does your church emphasize mentoring?

Never Too Late to Start

A few years ago, I watched an ESPN report of a one-hundred-year-old man named Orville Rogers setting the world record in his age group for the men's sixty-meter dash.[24] His age group was the 100–104 bracket, so he didn't have many competitors, but he beat the clock like no one had ever done. Rogers, whose story is told in the book *The Running Man: Flying High for the Glory of God*, lived for Christ as a World War II veteran, Southern Baptist missionary, and professional pilot.[25] When asked how he made it to one hundred, he replied, "No. 1, I'm a believer in our Lord, Jesus Christ. . . . No. 2, I had a loving wife."[26]

Let me tell you why the video clip fascinated me. I had heard stories about Orville from my pastoral mentor, Tom Elliff. Orville had been one of Tom's mentors for years, and they talked regularly until Orville's death at age 101—which means that when my mentor was in his seventies, he still had someone older discipling him. Through Tom's stories, I've had the benefit of Orville's teaching.

Orville didn't start running until age fifty, and he didn't start running competitively until he was ninety—but he *started somewhere* (even later in life), and he *did something*, running the race well (literally and figuratively) until the Lord called him across the finish line. He ran to the end with others—including me, by extension—still running behind him.

No matter how young or old you are, you can take the first steps today to lead your church toward becoming a disciple-making church. I challenge you to do *something* even before you read the next chapter.

PERSONAL REFLECTION QUESTIONS

1. Would you be willing to serve on your discipleship prayer team? How about starting it up (if it doesn't already exist)?
2. How would you describe the spiritual stage you're in now?
3. Name two or three believers who come to mind as potential mentees for you.

CHAPTER 4

Next Steps

I'M AN EDUCATOR AT HEART. I knew I wanted to be a teacher when I was in kindergarten, and I even set up a classroom in our playroom during my elementary school years. In my office, I still have a teacher's gradebook I bought when I was in fourth grade just because I wanted one.

I'm also a pastor at heart. I love the local church, and I rejoice in my opportunities to shepherd a group of people. I look forward to baptizing new believers, helping believers grow, and sending them out to do God's work. God's people, in spite of our ongoing sinfulness, really are the best. In the seminary and the local church, I get to serve with the best of the best.

Let me tell you, though, where my two worlds collide. In my seminary setting, my role as an administrator requires me to pay attention to core competencies, curriculum development, and ongoing assessment. We know what we want our students to be able to do by the time they graduate, and these goals are best expressed in our core competencies. For example, two of our desired competencies are biblical exposition (demonstrating the ability to properly and effectively communicate, interpret, and apply the Scriptures) and ministry preparation (demonstrating the knowledge, skills, and Christian disposition necessary for ministry and leadership in the church and the world).[1]

We always have room for improvement, but our goal is to move everything we do toward that end—every degree program, every course, every student learning outcome, every assignment designed to help our students become the equipped men and women we want them to be. In fact, our accreditors require us to give evidence of our effectiveness.

In my church world, though, I wish I could say that most congregations are equally organized and intentional. In educational lingo, many churches haven't determined what they want their disciples to be and do (core competencies), nor have they strategically planned to lead their members in that direction. Given both deficiencies, it's not surprising these churches also do little evaluation of what they accomplish. I hope this book helps churches begin to address these issues.

In the previous chapter, I offered several beginning steps in this direction. I trust you've taken some of these steps: assessing your own commitment to discipleship, enlisting a discipleship prayer team, growing comfortable with tackling a process with no end, and beginning to invest in two or three other believers. With those foundational pieces in place, the goal of this chapter is to suggest further steps toward accomplishing your church's discipleship goals.

Determine Your Church's "Disciple"

Remember Dave and Debbie, the composite examples of new believers in your community you want to lead to grow spiritually as disciples of Christ? If Saddleback Sam and Samantha are the image of the people you need to reach in your community, then Dave and Debbie are the type of disciples you want Sam and Samantha to become after you've reached them for Christ. It is by knowing the characteristics of the people you're trying to reach and the disciples you're trying to train up that you can then develop a "scorecard" to assess the growth of your church's members.

I don't know what process your church uses for developing disciples, but I can offer some thoughts to get you started on defining your desired characteristics.

The first one probably won't surprise you: Let the Word guide you as you determine what kind of disciple you want to produce. It is in God's Word that we learn what a disciple is. The Bible introduces us to the Great Commandment (Matthew 22:37-40) and the Great Commission (Matthew 28:18-20), and it describes for us the fruit of the Spirit (Galatians 5:22-23). As we've seen previously, every piece of the armor of God that disciples wear is somehow connected to the Sword of the Spirit, which is the Word of God (Ephesians 6:10-17). In Scripture, we learn about truth, righteousness, the gospel, faith, and salvation—all components of the armor that disciples must wear.

This point may sound simplistic, but defining your "disciple" must begin with studying and teaching what the Bible says about being a disciple. Perhaps chapter 2 of this book will help you with this. You might do your study with the elders of your church, with small group leaders, with your discipleship prayer team, or perhaps with an ad hoc team established to review your church's discipleship plan. In any case, you will also need to teach your entire congregation about discipleship in order to help them understand your goals and pathway. Just be sure to do it with the Word.

Second, don't try to define your church's "disciple" on your own. Jim Putman's thoughts are helpful here: "Do not try to shift your church as an individual. It's highly important that you shift as a team."[2] No one knows everything, and we all need the support and help of our brothers and sisters in Christ as we strategize for the future of our congregations. I confess my own tendency as a pastor to try to do everything on my own, and I can look back and see numerous mistakes I could have avoided by seeking input from others. My failure to lead my congregations as 1 Corinthians 12 churches—that is, helping them determine their place in the local church and equipping them to do their ministries—has sometimes led to unnecessary conflict. I don't want that to happen in your church as you determine who your disciples are.

Indeed, being a lone ranger leader not only ignores the inherent value of the body of Christ and its plurality of gifted individuals, but it is simply not wise leadership. Consider Thom Rainer's words about this concern: "Perhaps there was a day when change was relatively slow enough that one person could be fairly effective in leading change. But as we experience technological, societal, cultural, and economic change faster than ever, the solo act just does not cut it. Lone Ranger leaders are not good change leaders."[3] Don't be one of those leaders, especially as you address the issue of leading every member to be a faithful disciple of Christ.

How you accomplish this task may depend in part on your church's polity. But I suggest that you establish an ad hoc team of leaders who represent your church (that is, men and women, younger and older, newer and longer-term members, staff and laity) to work through this process, even if your polity requires final approval by another group. You will be discipling this ad hoc team as you lead them, and gaining the buy-in of a strong cross-representation of your church will help you in the long run. Learn together what a disciple is, and then teach others.

Third, learn from others who have already wrestled with the issue of discipleship development in the church. My missiological side encourages you to contextualize your approach to your church; but that commitment doesn't mean you must start from scratch. If you're aware of others who have started this process, learn from them. Contact them. Ask questions. Ask them to pray for you and your church. Indeed, this principle is important enough that I have included another section below that provides some examples. I hope they're helpful to you.

You might also consider inviting someone who has tackled this issue to help guide your ad hoc team through the process. Sometimes, a congregation will hear an outsider more readily than an insider, even when both say the exact same thing. Consider using another local church pastor, a denominational leader, or even a seminary professor to teach your team about developing your discipleship plan. Given the growth of digital delivery systems, don't limit yourself to local options as you seek someone to walk with you.

Fourth, make sure you continually keep your discipleship plans and goals in front of your congregation so they are reminded regularly of what you want them to become. If you go through the work to develop a plan for discipleship but no one knows about the goals, the work may be for naught. Explain your discipleship plan in your church's membership class. Review it in your church's business or family meetings. As you enlist new workers, remind them of your church's overall goal to produce the type of disciple you've defined, and help them to see how their volunteer efforts will contribute to that goal. Verify that potential staff hires are on board with this commitment to produce disciples. If you offer an annual State of the Church report, include—and emphasize—the results of your church's discipleship efforts.

EVALUATION FOR YOUR CHURCH

1. Does your church already have a model disciple in view?
2. If not, what would be the process for developing a model?

Don't Reinvent the Wheel If You Don't Have To

I understand those who advise church leaders not to try to duplicate what other churches are doing. Every church is different. Every context is specific. Every leader is unique. When we try to transplant somebody else's strategy into our context, failure often awaits. Daniel Im reminds us that when we try to change a declining church, "The solution isn't to look down the street and copy the nearby megachurch."[4] I agree, but I also affirm Im's next statement: "Nor is it to blow everything up and start from scratch. And by all means, staying the same is not an option either."[5]

We must indeed contextualize our disciplemaking strategies in our local churches, but that doesn't mean we can't learn from others who have considered the question, "Who or what is a disciple of Jesus?" For example, Jim Putman and his Real Life Ministries define a disciple as one who is

- following Christ (head),
- being changed by Christ (heart), and
- committed to the mission of Christ (hands).[6]

As their church members lead other believers to grow, they progressively guide them by a methodology they call "SCMD" (share, connect, minister, disciple) that models what Jesus did:

> For us in this day and age, it means that we *share* our lives with people. As we do, we share the gospel with them. Those who accept the message, we *connect* with, and as we do, we help them connect with Christ and with other believers. As we do life with these new disciples, we help supply a place for them to learn how to *minister* in Jesus' name. Finally, when they are ready, we release them to *disciple* others.[7]

With this goal in mind, they know what they want their disciple to be. Genuine disciples of Christ should love the lost, get to know them, and share the gospel with them. They should be involved in a small group to connect with other believers, and they should be inviting others to join the group. Next, they should be ministering by using their spiritual gifts in the body of Christ. Finally, disciples should be reproducing themselves and helping to raise up new disciplemaking leaders. The leaders of the church work to develop ministries that align with that vision, recognizing that "the most important scorecard for success is how many mature disciples your church has developed."[8]

Greg Ogden similarly looks at biblical marks of a disciple, and he concludes that a disciple

1. Is a *proactive* minister rather than a passive one. That is, a disciple is not a passive spectator; he is actively involved in his church through using his gifts.

2. Lives a *disciplined* life rather than a casual one. He serves Christ with the vigor of an athlete, making certain that spiritual disciplines are a component of his life.

3. Practices *holistic* rather than private discipleship. The disciple practices his faith in his home, his family, his church, his workplace; he allows his commitment to Christ to influence every domain of his life.

4. Lives a life *transformed* by the gospel rather than conformed to culture. He stands counterculturally by living according to God's standards.

5. Views the church as *essential* rather than optional. He sees the body of Christ as integral to God's plan, and he understands he must be part of it.

6. Is biblically *informed* rather than illiterate. He loves the Scriptures, knows them, and follows them.

7. Is an *active* witness rather than inactive. The disciple tells the Good News widely and freely.[9]

These characteristics provide a grid to evaluate whether a church is producing disciples. Disciples use their gifts, model Christ in their lives, exhibit godliness in a nonbelieving culture, love and support the church, know and follow God's Word, and share the gospel with others. Our responsibility as leaders is to strive to close the gap between this biblical standard and the reality of the church today.[10]

In my book *Membership Matters*, I list six categories to describe a disciple.[11] Some of these categories and applications overlap, but that's inevitable when you're talking about a discipled lifestyle.

1. **Knowledge.** Disciples need to *know* things like basic Bible organization, church doctrine and structure, hermeneutics (how to interpret the Bible), and the church's history and vision. They hear and follow Jesus' words: "You must love the LORD your God with all your heart, all your soul, and all your mind" (Matthew 22:37).

2. **Spiritual disciplines.** Opinions differ on how many spiritual disciplines there are, but I would include at least reading the Bible, praying, fasting, giving, serving, and memorizing Scripture. Disciples show their love for God by spending time with him; they follow Paul's command to Timothy to "train yourself to be godly" (1 Timothy 4:7).

3. **Theology.** What a disciple believes matters. Disciples should know basic biblical beliefs, and they should be able to explain the faith to others. New Testament scholar Wayne Grudem points out that they should grow to understand that studying theology "enables us to teach ourselves and others what the whole Bible says, thus fulfilling the second part of the Great Commission" (Matthew 28:20).[12]

4. **Ministry.** Disciples should serve in the church and the community, and love their neighbors and the nations. In the ministry category, I include evangelism, spiritual gifts discovery, and specific ministry preparation. Disciples understand where they fit in the local body of Christ and serve accordingly; they know that "a spiritual gift is given to each of us so we can help each other" (1 Corinthians 12:7).

5. **Participation.** This category may be the one most believers consider when they think of what disciples do.

Disciples should participate in the church's worship services, small groups, individual ministries, accountability groups (or partners), and equipping events. Because the Great Commission requires reaching the nations, I also include some kind of participation in supporting missions. Disciples may not be able to participate in every event or program the church offers, but they understand the importance of being with the people of God: "Let us think of ways to motivate one another to acts of love and good works. And let us not neglect our meeting together, as some people do, but encourage one another, especially now that the day of his return is drawing near" (Hebrews 10:24-25).

6. **Lifestyle.** Disciples of Christ imitate him in every area of their lives. They successfully fight temptation, forsake patterns of sin, build healthy relationships, and exhibit their "new lives" (Romans 6:4). They do what the apostle Paul commanded: "Throw off your old sinful nature and your former way of life, which is corrupted by lust and deception. Instead, let the Spirit renew your thoughts and attitudes. Put on your new nature, created to be like God—truly righteous and holy" (Ephesians 4:22-24).

Having a model like this is a good step toward developing a strategic plan for discipleship. It can guide your planning and your assessment.

Recognize Stages of Christian Growth

I wish you could have met my mom. She became a believer at age seventy-nine, and I had the privilege of baptizing her. It was one of the highlights of my ministry when she came out of the water and hugged my neck not only as her son, but also as her brother in Christ. No words could ever capture my joy on that day.

Just as much fun, though, was watching my mom grow in the Lord. Actually, she lived only six months after she became a believer, but they were exciting months indeed. She read her Bible for the first time, received her first women's Bible study curriculum, and even began serving as a volunteer in a ministry my brother leads. Her baby steps quickly became very small toddler steps.

Mom continually wanted to know the next right steps for her to grow. It was all new to her, so she didn't know—and she was not the least bit ashamed to ask for help. She asked questions and made statements that reminded us she was still young in her faith.

"Are you sure God will forgive me?"

"Can you really get saved late in life?"

"How can I understand the Bible?"

"I didn't know the Bible teaches that."

"What if I'm uncomfortable going to church?"

Mom wanted to live her Christianity well, so she regularly asked for guidance. Her status as great-grandma, grandma, and mom didn't keep her from seeking help. Even up to two days before her unexpected death, she was asking about possible next steps in her growth.

My mom was at the baby stage of her faith, just beginning to feed on the milk of the Word. New Testament writers sharply criticize believers who remain at the baby stage when they should be growing (e.g., 1 Corinthians 3:2; Hebrews 4:12-13), but Peter uses an infant to illustrate how believers ought to crave God's Word: "Like newborn babies, you must crave pure spiritual milk so that you will grow into a full experience of salvation" (1 Peter 2:2). We

DISCIPLE

are to yearn for more of God's Word so that we may grow in our salvation, recognizing that we "must grow in the grace and knowledge of our Lord and Savior Jesus Christ" (2 Peter 3:18). My mom was crying out to know more, even as a new child of God.

Knowing where my mom was in her faith mattered as we considered ways to help her grow. How I would have discipled my mom would be different from how I disciple most of my seminary students. Generally, my students are further along in their faith than my mom was. At a minimum, their questions are different. My students are not asking so much *what* they should do; they're asking *how* they should do what they know they should do. They're sometimes dealing with hidden sin, whereas my mom was still learning what constitutes sin. My mom didn't even own a Bible until my brother bought her one, but my students often come from homes with more Bibles than people.

When I think of some of the questions I ask those who mentor me at my stage of life, the discipling situation again looks different. I don't struggle with daily reading the Word, but I have asked for guidance in knowing how to avoid a "checklist" devotional time. I need brothers in Christ who help me consider God's will so I don't let my heart deceive me. I need them to show me how to continue to love my wife, Pam, in ways that honor her and proclaim the gospel no matter how long we're married. As I get older, I also increasingly want to know from older believers how to make sure I finish well.

Knowing where those we disciple are in their spiritual walk, in addition to knowing where we are personally, is an important part of disciplemaking. Where we start in discipling somebody depends upon where that believer is in his or her Christian journey.

Again, we don't need to reinvent the wheel when considering stages of discipleship. Aubrey Malphurs, for example, categorizes spiritual stages quite simply, and he argues that Jesus "expects his entire church (not simply a few passionate disciple makers) to move people along a maturity or disciple-making continuum, from prebirth (unbelief) to the new birth (belief) and then to maturity."[13]

MALPHURS'S DISCIPLEMAKING CONTINUUM

Nondisciple	New Disciple	Growing Disciple
Pre-birth	New birth	Maturity
(unbelief)	(belief)	(growth)

More fully developed is Real Life Ministries' "Life Stages of a Disciple."[14] In stage 1, *spiritually dead*, potential disciples are still nonbelievers. They are dead in their sin (Ephesians 2:1) and destined for eternal judgment apart from a relationship with Christ. In stage 2, the *spiritual infant* stage, new believers are excited and zealous, but not yet knowledgeable about faith. Stage 3, the *spiritual child* stage, is characterized by believers who are beginning to learn their faith, but who sometimes still reflect their childlikeness and self-centeredness. In stage 4, the *spiritual young adult* stage, believers have grown significantly and want to serve in the church. They still need discipleship, though, and they're typically not ready yet to "reproduce disciples who can make disciples."[15]

Getting to stage 5, the *parenting* stage, is the goal. In this stage, mature believers are not just longer-term believers; they are believers who are intentionally reproducing themselves through disciplemaking. For that reason, Jim Putman uses the word *parent* rather than *adult*—that is, an adult might be someone who claims to be mature but is not reproducing himself or herself like a parent does. Putman goes so far as to say that a believer who is not reproducing is not really mature in faith.[16] I suspect that assessment would bother a lot of church members in America!

Why does it matter that we know these stages? On the one hand, this understanding should remind those of us who claim to be mature that we did not start in this place. We were all lost once. We were all spiritual infants once. If we have grown at all through the stages, it is because God has graciously used his Word, his Spirit, and his people to grow us. It is not because we are more significant in the body of Christ. As I've said before, I've known some infant believers who are much more of a threat to Satan than other "mature" believers who have lost their fire.

On the other hand, this use of stages should help us grant grace, patience, and forgiveness to younger-stage believers who are still learning to walk. Our goal is to help them move in the right direction, but they may not move as quickly as we would like. They may fail even after we have spent significant time with them. They may not always listen, and they may not do what we encourage them to do. Giving up on them, though, is not the answer. They're still young in their faith, so they need our ongoing instruction—and our patience.

Next, I use the stages to determine where to begin with someone I'm discipling. Simply asking people where they see themselves on the list of stages can be enlightening. Some see themselves as quite mature, while others see themselves almost as nonbelievers still. It's not uncommon that I disagree with someone's own assessment, but it's a starting point. We can work together from there to determine the next steps in the discipling relationship.

Further, knowing the stages can be significant as churches enlist workers in the congregation. Imagine this scenario, for example: An adult believer who recently met Christ has joined the church. She's joyous in her new faith, and she wants to serve in any way she can. She doesn't want to miss anything God may have for her. She is a trained educator in the local school system, and it's obvious she loves to teach. When she completed a spiritual gifts inventory in the church's membership class, the gift of teaching ranked first. A trained, experienced, gifted, willing teacher has joined the church.

As it happens, this church has struggled finding teachers for adult small groups. *Maybe she's an answer to our prayer*, some in the church think. Should the church enlist her for one of those positions to teach the Bible? Many churches would. But based on her stage of spiritual growth, that's a problematic decision. As an infant in her Christian experience, this sister is not ready to teach in an official capacity. The danger is that we might set up this young, undiscipled believer for a fall into pride—or worse yet, she might (even unintentionally) teach a wrong understanding of the Scriptures. Both problems can happen, of course, even to more mature believers, but the risk is higher with an infant believer.

Here's one more way the stages are helpful to me: They remind me to be careful in assessing where believers are. A few years ago, I wrote a blog post titled "10 Differences between Baby Believers and Believers Who Are Babies."[17] I realize that such categorizations always have exceptions, but I was trying to point out differences between infant believers and those who think they're mature but aren't.

1. Baby believers are hungry for God and his Word; believers who are babies think they already know God's Word.

2. Baby believers are teachable; believers who are babies complain when they don't get to teach.

3. Baby believers tell others about Jesus; believers who are babies tell others about themselves.

4. Baby believers cry when they're hurt because they don't understand; believers who are babies whine when they don't get their way.

5. Baby believers look up to their church's spiritual leaders; believers who are babies expect others to look up to them.

6. Baby believers admit they don't know something; believers who are babies tend to make up something rather than admit their ignorance.

7. Baby believers rejoice when others do well; believers who are babies become jealous of those who do well.

8. Baby believers tend to shy away from the limelight; believers who are babies expect attention.

9. Baby believers struggle with sin, but they want to fight it; believers who are babies make excuses for their sin.

10. Baby believers tend to be joyful, no matter what happens; believers who are babies tend to be angry and unpleasant—no matter what happens.

Again, I realize these generalizations may be overstated at times, but I trust you understand the contrasts. We have all kinds of people in our churches, and they are at different stages of their Christian walk. Some are still young, and they know it. Others are immature, but they don't recognize it. Many, we hope, are growing in their walk. Knowing what stage our church members are in is critical to discipling them.

It might surprise you, though, how this understanding of stages helps me as I lead others. When I have to deal with someone who appears to be a believer who is a baby—a whiner, perhaps—I first think, *I wonder whether anyone has ever discipled this believer—or if others may have given him or her authority in the church too soon.* It might be that this immature church member has always walked alone because no one has invested in him or her. I will still have to deal appropriately with the immaturity, but understanding the stages helps me be patient and thoughtful in my response.

EVALUATION FOR YOUR CHURCH
1. Using Putman's five stages, where do you think most members of your church are?
2. What strengths does your church have that will help them make other disciples?

Build on What's Already Happening in Your Church

To be honest, I wrote that heading with a bit of concern. Given that so many churches are not disciplemaking churches, I'm not sure I want to emphasize this point too much. Will Mancini makes the point that a church that is getting "great results" with their current model should work at maximizing what they're doing—but, he adds, that's "simply not the place that most of us need to expand our thinking."[18] Most churches need to change in order to do better disciplemaking. Still, I think there's something to be said for building on your church's current efforts. Approaching it that way can be less chaotic than simply starting over, and your members may be more inclined toward change if it's less dramatic.

I view discipleship as occurring at three levels, which should all be components of the disciplemaking process in your church:

1. **The corporate level.** Through all that takes place in worship services, we should be teaching believers to grow in their faith. This is likely the broadest level of our discipleship, but it is also difficult to walk personally with everyone sitting in our worship services.

2. **The small group level.** Almost every practitioner and writer I know who emphasizes discipleship also identifies small groups as a significant platform for that task. The size and purposes of the groups vary by church, but they're generally the primary place to build life-on-life relationships; hence, groups are the "backbone for discipleship."[19] They are also the best place to ask the types of scorecard questions we don't often ask:

   - What percentage of our members are reading the Bible regularly?
   - How many have been trained to share the gospel this year? How many have done it?
   - How are our members and their groups reaching out into the community?
   - How many members have taken a mission trip in the last year?
   - How many new leaders have we raised up this year?
   - What percentage of members know and use their spiritual gifts?
   - What percentage of fathers are intentionally leading their families in discipleship?
   - How many members are in a discipling relationship?

   We have to *know* our church body if we want to assess where they are spiritually, and a small group is usually the best place to do that.

3. **The mentoring level.** Mentoring is the most personal level, and it ideally leads to disciples who make other disciples. In many cases, accountability—a critical component of disciplemaking—is deeper at this level than any other.

Most churches already have the first two components in place, even if they're not always done well. They have at least some structure in place to move forward if someone leads them well. If you want to improve your church's disciplemaking, it may be that you will have to start where your church is and try to improve what you are currently doing. Build strategically and intentionally on components already in place.

Let me give you two simple examples. First, assume that my church has made a commitment to teaching basic doctrine (a knowledge goal). Here are some possible ways I might lead change in this direction using our current options. I might plan a doctrinal sermon series each of the next three years. If I intentionally cover one doctrine each year while also pointing out doctrinal truths as I exposit the Word the rest of the year, I've taken a step in the right direction.

Our small groups might then plan to discuss the doctrine series when it's preached, or the church might plan another small group–based doctrinal study each year. Either way, the church is teaching doctrine at a more intimate level in small groups. Doing so also necessitates that we have equipped our small group leaders to facilitate doctrinal discussion, so we get to spend time with them first to prepare them. At a mentoring level, I would encourage my mentees to ask any doctrinal questions they still have.

Second, my church also plans to help our members discover and use their spiritual gifts (a ministry goal). One option would be for our pastors to lead an annual sermon series or a weekend conference to understand what these gifts are. Another option would be for our small groups to study spiritual gifts, work together to complete gifts inventories, evaluate each other's gifts and strengths for serving through the church, and help members get "plugged in" to a ministry that fits their gifting. As a mentor, I would likely want to dig more deeply into my disciples' giftedness, experiences, training, and calling to see how I might challenge them more to follow Christ. Regularly and wisely doing any one of these options (or a combination of all three) will help you meet one expectation of your church's disciples.

My goal here is to show that if we know what we want to accomplish in growing our church's discipleship focus, we can often improve what we're doing simply by planning more strategically. Plan events, activities, and trainings with great intentionality, connecting disciples with one another so that the puzzle looks right in the end. Think strategically in terms of *years* rather than weeks. Haphazard planning may lead to activity, but it seldom leads to disciples.

Define where you want your disciples to end up. Lead intentionally toward producing that desired outcome. Find out where you might strengthen and direct some of your current ministries by helping the participants see their role in producing disciples. Build accountability into the process, asking small group leaders and mentors to help you assess whether your church members are growing. Show your leaders where they fit in your church's disciplemaking process.

I'm convinced we can become stronger disciplemaking churches if we do a better job of putting the puzzle pieces together in an effective way. Start today by evaluating which pieces you have available right now, and plan more strategically to put these pieces together to build disciples.

Let's Win the Game

I am a fan of pro football. My team is the Cincinnati Bengals—which means I've been disappointed more than elated over the years (including the 2021–2022 season, though it was fun to root for them in the Super Bowl). I love watching football, and seldom does a Sunday go by during the season without my paying attention to at least one game.

Sometimes, I'll have the game on in the background while I'm doing something else, and I pay attention only when I hear the roar of a crowd or the excitement in an announcer's voice. That particularly happens when a team scores a touchdown. What I've learned, though, is that the excitement of an individual touchdown doesn't matter much if my team loses the game in the end. The goal is to win the game, not just get a touchdown.

I thought about that illustration when I read J. T. English's statement "Conversion is not the touchdown of the Christian life; it is the kickoff."[20] We celebrate the conversion of a nonbeliever, but our work as a church is far from over then. In many ways, it is just beginning—and it won't end until the Lord returns. I pray the Lord will grant you wisdom as you take the next steps to lead your church toward maturity and victory.

PERSONAL REFLECTION QUESTIONS

1. What characteristics do you want your church's disciples to have?
2. Where are you in your own spiritual walk? Are you still a baby believer? Or do you sometimes act like a believer who is a baby?
3. How might you help your church put the discipleship puzzle pieces together?

Conclusion

I AM WRITING this conclusion in Florida, where I'm visiting Disney World. Yesterday we spent time in the Toy Story Land section of Disney's Hollywood Studios. There, to my surprise, I saw large replicas of toys I played with as a child: Tinkertoys, Lincoln Logs, building blocks, Legos, and checkers. The toys in Disney were taller than I am, but they looked remarkably like the ones I remember.

I still recall stacking building blocks as high as I could reach. I tried to extend my Tinkertoy contraptions all the way across the room. I loved interlocking the Lincoln Logs to make cabins. With Legos, I could make almost anything I could envision. And the checkers—well, I built towers one piece at a time until they inevitably tilted and collapsed. It's surprising to me that I can still see in my mind some of the things I built more than five decades ago (and to be honest, I laugh at those images now because I'm hardly mechanically inclined today).

In all these examples from my childhood, I had the resources I needed. In fact, I usually dumped all the pieces on the floor first, and I typically had more than I needed to make what I wanted. All the toys were there for building stuff—and I had the fun job of putting them together the right way.

You are a part of what God is building. He is the one who builds the church, but you have a role in it. Whatever your position, your responsibility is to use your gifts and make disciples through your church. The good news is that you already have the resources you need to get the job done. You have God's Word, God's Spirit, and God's people.

God makes himself known to us through his Word. He lives in us through his Spirit. He loves us through his people. He calls us to follow him with abandon, and he promises to be with us all the way (Matthew 28:20). We have no reason not to do what he has called us to do.

God has called us to make disciples.

Each church might do that work differently, but our calling is the same. We are to teach others what God has taught us, and they are then to teach the next generations. We are to live like Jesus and challenge others to imitate us. We are to reach the world with the gospel so the nations might also become disciples. These responsibilities are huge, and we cannot accomplish them on our own. But God has given us what we need.

I don't know what steps your church needs to take to become a disciplemaking church. I do know that you can take some immediate steps (such as deepening your own walk with Christ and choosing to invest in others) to strengthen your church. Other steps may take longer to accomplish. You may need a longer-term vision to keep pressing your church to make disciples who live genuinely and passionately for Christ.

But you have what you need.

Get some church folks around you and start to pray. Seek God through his Word. Listen to his Spirit. Be with his people. Take a look at which puzzle pieces you already have available. Then take the next steps to put the puzzle together to build people up and make disciples for Jesus.

Whatever you do, don't leave the puzzle pieces lying on the floor.

Notes

INTRODUCTION

1. The Know Your Church Report is available at https://churchanswers.com/solutions/tools/know-your-church/.
2. See, for example, Thom S. Rainer, "Major New Research on Declining, Plateaued, and Growing Churches from Exponential and LifeWay Research," Church Answers blog, March 6, 2019, https://churchanswers.com/blog/major-new-research-on-declining-plateaued-and-growing-churches-from-exponential-and-lifeway-research/.
3. *The State of Discipleship: A Barna Report Produced in Partnership with The Navigators* (Colorado Springs, CO: Navigators, 2015).
4. Greg Ogden, *Transforming Discipleship: Making Disciples a Few at a Time* (Downers Grove, IL: InterVarsity, 2016), 22.
5. Chuck Lawless, "6 Reasons Churches Don't Disciple Well," June 9, 2020, https://chucklawless.com/2020/06/6-reasons-churches-dont-disciple-well/.
6. Chuck Lawless, *Membership Matters* (Grand Rapids, MI: Zondervan, 2005), 109.
7. Ed Stetzer and Thom S. Rainer, *Transformational Church* (Nashville, TN: B&H, 2010), 32.
8. J. T. English, *Deep Discipleship: How the Church Can Make Whole Disciples of Jesus* (Nashville, TN: B&H, 2020), 62.

CHAPTER 1: THE PROBLEM

1. For a similar progression, see Aubrey Malphurs, *Strategic Disciple Making* (Grand Rapids, MI: Baker, 2009), 18–19.
2. Chuck Lawless, "10 Results of Poor Discipleship in the Church," August 20, 2015, https://chucklawless.com/2015/08/10-results-of-poor-discipleship-in-the-church/.

3. Robert E. Coleman, *The Master Plan of Evangelism* (Grand Rapids, MI: Revell, 1993).

4. Rick Warren, *The Purpose Driven Church: Growth without Compromising Your Message and Mission* (Grand Rapids, MI: Zondervan, 1995).

5. Warren, *Purpose Driven Church*, 51. Italics in the original.

6. Warren, *Purpose Driven Church*, 144.

7. Warren, *Purpose Driven Church*, 144.

8. Warren, *Purpose Driven Church*, 336.

9. Warren, *Purpose Driven Church*, 145.

10. Warren, *Purpose Driven Church*, 170.

11. Warren, *Purpose Driven Church*, 170.

12. "Dave" was first introduced in Chuck Lawless, *Membership Matters* (Grand Rapids, MI: Zondervan, 2005), 145–148.

13. Will Mancini, *Innovating Discipleship: Four Paths to Real Discipleship Results* (n. p., Church Unique Intentional Leader Series, 2013), 14.

14. Aubrey Malphurs, *Strategic Disciple Making: A Practical Tool for Successful Ministry* (Grand Rapids, MI: Baker, 2009), 77.

15. See Dean M. Kelly, *Why Conservative Churches Are Growing: A Study in Sociology of Religion* (San Francisco: Harper & Row, 1972); Thom S. Rainer, *High Expectations: The Remarkable Secret for Keeping People in Your Church* (Nashville, TN: B&H, 1999).

16. Adapted from Chuck Lawless, "9 Reasons Why Churches Think They're Disciplemaking Churches When They May Not Be," March 11, 2020, https://chucklawless.com/2020/03/9-reasons-why-churches-think-theyre -disciplemaking-churches-when-they-may-not-be/.

17. George Barna, "Research Shows That Spiritual Maturity Process Should Start at a Young Age," November 17, 2003, https://www.barna .com/research/research-shows-that-spiritual-maturity-process-should -start-at-a-young-age/; Howard Culbertson, "At What Age Do Americans Become Christians?" http://home.snu.edu/~hculbert/ages.htm.

18. Robby Gallaty, *Rediscovering Discipleship: Making Jesus' Final Words Our First Work* (Grand Rapids, MI: Zondervan, 2015), 38. Italics in the original.

19. Gallaty, *Rediscovering Discipleship*, 40.

20. Bill Hull, *The Disciple-Making Church: Leading a Body of Believers on the Journey of Faith* (Grand Rapids, MI: Baker, 2010), 56.

CHAPTER 2: WHAT EXACTLY IS A DISCIPLE?

1. Mark Liederbach, *Chasing Infinity: Discipleship as the Pursuit of Infinite Treasure* (Orlando, FL: Cru Press, 2017), 12.

2. Liederbach, *Chasing Infinity*, 12.

3. Liederbach, *Chasing Infinity*, 12.

4. Rick Warren, *The Purpose Driven Church: Growth without Compromising Your Message and Mission* (Grand Rapids, MI: Zondervan, 1995), 103.

5. J. T. English, *Deep Discipleship: How the Church Can Make Whole Disciples of Jesus* (Nashville, TN: B&H, 2020), 161–162.

6. John R. W. Stott, *God's New Society: The Message of Ephesians* (Downers Grove, IL: InterVarsity, 1979), 137.

7. Aubrey Malphurs, *Strategic Disciple Making: A Practical Tool for Successful Ministry* (Grand Rapids, MI: Baker, 2009), 31.

8. Michael J. Wilkins, *Following the Master: A Biblical Theology of Discipleship* (Grand Rapids, MI: Zondervan, 1992), 212.

9. Colin G. Kruse, *John*, Tyndale New Testament Commentaries, vol. 4 (Downers Grove, IL: InterVarsity Press, 2003), 207.

10. Timothy George, *Galatians*, The New American Commentary, vol. 30 (Nashville, TN: B&H, 1994), 400.

11. Donald K. Campbell, "Galatians," in John F. Walvoord and Roy B. Zuck, eds., *The Bible Knowledge Commentary: An Exposition of the Scriptures*, vol. 2 (Wheaton, IL: Victor Books, 1985), 608.

12. Campbell, "Galatians," 608.

13. Campbell, "Galatians," 608.

14. William F. Cook III and Chuck Lawless, *Spiritual Warfare in the Storyline of Scripture: A Biblical, Theological, and Practical Approach* (Nashville, TN: B&H, 2019), 324.

15. See Cook and Lawless, *Spiritual Warfare*, 225–227.

16. Chuck Lawless, *Discipled Warriors* (Grand Rapids, MI: Kregel, 2002), 29.

17. For more detail, see Cook and Lawless, *Spiritual Warfare*.

18. G. L. Borchert, *John 12–21*, The New American Commentary, vol. 25 (Nashville, TN: B&H, 2002), 99.

19. Charles M. Sheldon, *In His Steps* (Sahuarita, AZ: Serenity, 2010).

20. David Prior, *The Message of 1 Corinthians: Life in the Local Church* (Downers Grove, IL: InterVarsity, 1985), 68.

21. Scholars debate the origin of this phrase.

CHAPTER 3: GETTING STARTED AS A DISCIPLEMAKING CHURCH

1. Kevin DeYoung, *Just Do Something: A Liberating Approach to Finding God's Will* (Chicago: Moody, 2009).

2. Chuck Lawless, *The Potential and Power of Prayer* (Carol Stream, IL: Tyndale Momentum, 2022).

3. Greg Ogden, *Transforming Discipleship: Making Disciples a Few at a Time* (Downers Grove, IL: InterVarsity, 2016), 208.

4. Chuck Lawless, "10 Reasons Church Leaders Should Admit It If They've Never Been Discipled," October 22, 2015, https://chucklawless.com /2015/10/5665/.

5. Chuck Lawless, *Mentor: How Along-the-Way Discipleship Will Change Your Life* (Nashville, TN: Lifeway, 2011), 73–74.
6. Adapted from Chuck Lawless, "Why You Need a Mentor, and How to Find One," June 27, 2019, https://chucklawless.com/2019/06/why-you-need-a-mentor-and-how-to-find-one/.
7. Jim Putman and Bobby Harrington with Robert E. Coleman, *DiscipleShift: Five Steps That Help Your Church to Make Disciples Who Make Disciples* (Grand Rapids, MI: Zondervan, 2013), 110.
8. Putman and Harrington, *DiscipleShift*, 114.
9. Putman and Harrington, *DiscipleShift*, 114.
10. Ogden, *Transforming Discipleship*, 115.
11. J. T. English, *Deep Discipleship: How the Church Can Make Whole Disciples* (Nashville, TN: B&H, 2020), 94, 111.
12. John Mark Terry and J. D. Payne, *Developing a Strategy for Missions: A Biblical, Historical, and Cultural Introduction* (Grand Rapids, MI: Baker Academic, 2013), 14.
13. Charles Spurgeon, "The Two Guards: Praying and Watching," a sermon delivered at Metropolitan Tabernacle, Newington, UK, July 24, 1809, https://www.blueletterbible.org/Comm/spurgeon_charles/sermons/2254.cfm.
14. Chuck Lawless, *Discipled Warriors: Growing Healthy Churches That Are Equipped for Spiritual Warfare* (Grand Rapids, MI: Kregel, 2002), 164.
15. Ed Stetzer and Thom S. Rainer, *Transformational Church: Creating a New Scorecard for Congregations* (Nashville, TN: B&H, 2010), 36.
16. Jim Collins, *Good to Great: Why Some Companies Make the Leap and Others Don't* (New York: HarperCollins, 2001), 13.
17. Robert Coleman and Bobby Harrington with Josh Patrick, *Revisiting the Master Plan of Evangelism: Why Jesus' Discipleship Method Is Still the Best Today* (Exponential Resources, 2014), 12–13, https://discipleship.org/wp-content/uploads/2016/08/Revisiting-the-Master-Plan-of-Evangelism.pdf.
18. Daniel Im, *No Silver Bullets: Five Small Shifts That Will Transform Your Ministry* (Nashville, TN: B&H, 2017), 39.
19. Chuck Lawless, *Mentor: How Along-the-Way Discipleship Will Change Your Life* (Nashville, TN: Lifeway, 2011), 10.
20. Howard Hendricks and William Hendricks, *As Iron Sharpens Iron: Building Character in a Mentoring Relationship* (Chicago: Moody, 1995), 78.
21. Hendricks and Hendricks, *As Iron Sharpens Iron*, 78.
22. See, for example, Tim Henderson, "The Right People for Discipleship," accessed February 17, 2022, https://www.cru.org/us/en/train-and-grow/help-others-grow/discipleship/the-right-people-for-discipleship.html.
23. Chuck Lawless, *Mentor*, 73–74.
24. Alex Butler, "Orville Rogers: 100-Year-Old Man Sets World Record in

Indoor Track," UPI, March 18, 2018, https://www.upi.com/Sports_News
/2018/03/18/Orville-Rogers-100-year-old-man-sets-world-record-in
-indoor-track/2441521347880/.

25. See Orville Rogers, *The Running Man: Flying High for the Glory of God* (Franklin, TN: Clovercroft, 2016).

26. Kip Hill, "At 100, Orville Rogers Misses World Record Chance in Spokane but Hopes for Strong Weekend on Track," *Spokesman-Review*, July 27, 2018, https://www.spokesman.com/stories/2018/jul/27/at-100-orville -rogers-misses-world-record-chance-i/.

CHAPTER 4: NEXT STEPS

1. *2021–2022 Student Handbook*, Southeastern Baptist Theological Seminary, 2.

2. Jim Putman and Bobby Harrington with Robert E. Coleman, *DiscipleShift: Five Steps That Help Your Church Make Disciples Who Make Disciples* (Grand Rapids, MI: Zondervan, 2013), 217.

3. Thom S. Rainer, *Who Moved My Pulpit?: Leading Change in the Church* (Nashville, TN: B&H, 2016), Kindle location 664–670.

4. Daniel Im, *No Silver Bullets: Five Small Shifts That Will Transform Your Ministry* (Nashville, TN: B&H, 2017), 14.

5. Im, *No Silver Bullets*, 14.

6. Putman and Harrington, *DiscipleShift*, 51.

7. Putman and Harrington, *DiscipleShift*, 166. Italics in original.

8. Putman and Harrington, *DiscipleShift*, 210.

9. Greg Ogden, *Transforming Discipleship: Making Disciples a Few at a Time* (Downers Grove, IL: InterVarsity, 2016), 24.

10. Ogden, *Transforming Discipleship*, 38.

11. Adapted from Chuck Lawless, *Membership Matters: Insights from Effective Churches on New Member Classes and Assimilation* (Grand Rapids, MI: Zondervan, 2005), 147.

12. Wayne Grudem, *Systematic Theology: An Introduction to Biblical Doctrine* (Grand Rapids, MI: Zondervan, 1994), 27–28.

13. Aubrey Malphurs, *Strategic Disciple Making: A Practical Tool for Successful Ministry* (Grand Rapids, MI: Baker, 2009), 20.

14. Jim Putman, *Real-Life Discipleship* (Colorado Springs, CO: NavPress, 2010), 40–43.

15. Putman and Harrington, *DiscipleShift*, 34–35.

16. Putman, *Real-Life Discipleship*, 42.

17. Chuck Lawless, "10 Differences between Baby Believers and Believers Who Are Babies," December 14, 2011, https://chucklawless.com/2017/12/10 -differences-between-baby-believers-and-believers-who-are-babies/.

18. Will Mancini, *Innovating Discipleship: Four Paths to Real Discipleship Results* (Church Unique Intentional Leader Series Book 1), 52.

19. Putman and Harrington, *DiscipleShift*, 186.

20. J. T. English, *Deep Discipleship: How the Church Can Make Whole Disciples* (Nashville, TN: B&H, 2020), 62.

About the Author

Chuck Lawless currently serves as professor of evangelism and missions, dean of doctoral studies, and vice president for spiritual formation and ministry centers at Southeastern Seminary. He served as a senior pastor for fourteen years and an interim pastor in several churches.

Dr. Lawless has authored or edited ten books, including *Spiritual Warfare, Discipled Warriors, Making Disciples through Mentoring, Serving in Your Church's Prayer Ministry*, and *Spiritual Warfare in the Storyline of Scripture*. Dr. Lawless speaks extensively around the country. He and his wife, Pam, live in Wake Forest, North Carolina.